David

A man after God's heart

Volume 1

David

A man after God's heart

Volume 1

When God is with you,
Wherever you are, you will succeed

E. A. Adeboye

Published by RoperPenberthy Publishing Ltd
Springfield House, 23 Oatlands Drive, Weybridge, Surrey KT13 9LZ

Text copyright © E A Adeboye, 2010

All Bible quotations are from the Authorised King James Version of the Holy Bible.

This Edition published 2010
First published February 1998
Reprint September 2009

ISBN 978 1 903905 64 7

Initially published by Christ the Redeemer's Ministries
Contact Address:
Redeemed Christian Church of God, Central Office UK, Redemption House, Station Road, Knebworth, Hertfordshire SG3 6AT United Kingdom

Cover design by Audri Coleman

Typeset by Avocet Typeset, Chilton, Aylesbury, Buckinghamshire

Printed in India by Imprint Digital

Table of Contents

Preface

Many of us think of David as a king, but, David was also a prophet, a shepherd and a dancer. The first time we heard about David was because God was angry with someone. This teaches us one important lesson right from the outset – God always has a substitute. Also, we learn that God can reject people. When God rejects a man, what follows next is his destruction. The common feature in almost all men rejected by God is pride. God resists the proud. Furthermore, the Lord's decision is always final. God is not a democrat. If it were to be by vote. David would never have become king. God is an autocrat.

The Almighty God said that David was the man of His choice. What kind of person will God choose? God will choose the foolish. God will choose the weak. God will choose the people that are regarded as nothing. If you are already wise, it will be difficult for God to use you. A foolish man is likely to do whatever God says. If he needs wisdom for anything at all, he will ask God and God will give him divine wisdom. If you are already strong, how can God give you strength? If you are already something, it becomes difficult for God to use you. The representatives of God are always given the power of God. If you will ever be chosen by God, you must receive power.

When the Holy Spirit came on David, He departed from Saul and demons took over. If you allow God to fill you with the Holy Spirit, you will begin to see the glory of God even while you are still here on earth. On the other hand it is dangerous to be discarded by God. It is far better never to have been used by God in the first place. Once God discards you, the devil will move in.

David was also a valiant man. The people that know God shall be strong and they shall do exploits to be strong, therefore, all you need to do is to know God. All power belongs to God. If the Almighty God is dwelling in you, inevitably, you will be very strong. David was a handsome person but God did not choose him because he was handsome. Physical beauty has very little to do with God's dealings. The kind of beauty that God in is interested in inner beauty. God is not affected by outward beauty that does not come from inner beauty.

We are also told that God was with David. When God is with someone, several things follow. The first thing is that He is backing you up. When God is backing you up, opposition will crumble. Divine protection is also guaranteed if God is with you; any fire that the enemy may prepare for you will only burn the cords that bind you. If God is with you, when the time comes to depart, you will sing all the way home.

When God is with you, it follows that you must be just. When God is with you, anybody you meet will be blessed. Divine favour also follows if God is with you. When God is with you, you will begin to rise up. If God is with you, wherever you are, you will succeed. If God withdraws from you, trouble awaits you. Do not lose Christ or you will lose everything. God is more than sufficient. If you are finding things difficult now, yet keep holding on to God, you will surely have the last laugh.

You can rely on any promise of the Almighty God. God has promised that you will be more than a conqueror. Do not play with anything that is contrary to the will of God. Flee from anything that will provoke the anger of God. If you are a backslider, return to your Lord; go and get fresh fire from God.

This book covers the events of the life of David from 1 Samuel 16 to 1 Samuel 20. Happy reading.

Pastor E. A. Adeboye

Chapter 1

DAVID WAS MUCH MORE THAN A KING

Of all the Old Testament saints, there is hardly anyone that who is closer to a New Testament Christian than David. He was almost everything a Christian is expected to be.

Many of us know David was a king. However, he was much more than a king. In 1 Samuel 16:17-18, the Bible says:

> *"And Saul said unto his servants, Provide me now a man that can play well, and bring him to me. Then answered one of the servants, and said, Behold, I have seen a son of Jesse the Bethlehemite, that is cunning in playing, and a mighty valiant man, and a man of war, and prudent in matters, and a comely person, and the Lord is with him."*

At the time King Saul was suffering from a bout of insanity and his servants came to him and asked if he should find a good musician who would be play to him when evil spirits tormented him. King Saul agreed to this idea and David was presented to him. We observe that David was not an ordinary musician. He was a talented performer. David was also a warrior. In 1 Samuel 17:32, the Bible tells us:

"And David said to Saul, Let no man's heart fail because of him; they servant will go and fight with this Philistine."

At this time, Goliath was terrorising the people and nobody was willing to challenge him. When David came, he said he was going to fight Goliath.

In 1 Samuel 30:7-8, the Bible tells us more about David:

"And David said to Abiathar the priest, Ahimelech's son, I pray thee, bring me hither the ephod. And Abiathar brought thither the ephod to David. And David enquired at the LORD, saying, shall I pursue after this troop? shall I overtake them? And he answered him, Pursue: for thou shalt surely overtake them, and without fail recover all."

David and his men were at the time in the service of the Philistine King Achish of Gath. The Philistines were about to join battle with the Israelites, but the other Philistine lords were afraid that David might fight against them instead of fighting for them. They said David and his men should be sent back. The king agreed.

While they were away, another army had come and plundered Ziklag, where David and his men were living. They took wives, children and property. His men began to weep and in fact, they wanted to stone David. David then decided to seek the face of the Lord. He called the priests and asked for the ephod. The ephod was what the priests wore when they went to seek the face of the Lord.

Under normal circumstances, a king should not perform the duties of a priest. This was one of the sins of King Saul did that brought on him the wrath of God. In the case of David, however, he was not just a king but he was also a priest. He sought the face of the Lord and God answered him.

More than this, David was also a prophet. The opening verse of Psalm 22 written by David, is prophetic:

"My God, my God, why hast thou forsaken me? Why art thou so far from helping me, and from the word of my roaring?"

This was the statement that Jesus Christ repeated when He was on the cross. David prophesied what would happen one thousand years ahead. As a matter of fact Psalm 22, 23 and 24 are prophecies concerning the Lord Jesus Christ given by David. In Psalm 22, he talked about Jesus Christ as the One who would come to suffer. In Psalm 23, he talked about Jesus Christ as the One who would care for His people. In Psalm 24, he talked about the Second Coming of Jesus Christ.

David was also a shepherd. In 1 Samuel 16:11, the Bible says:

"And Samuel said unto Jesse, Are here all thy children? And he said, there remaineth yet the youngest, and, behold, he keepeth the sheep. And Samuel said unto Jesse, send and fetch him: for we will not sit down till he come hither."

In addition to all the above, David, was an anointed one. In 1 Samuel 16:13, the Bible says:

"Then Samuel took the horn of oil, and anointed him in the midst of his brethren: and the spirit of the LORD came upon David from that day forward. So Samuel rose up, and went to Ramah."

David was also a dancer. 2 Samuel 6:14-16 confirms this fact:

"And David danced before the LORD with all his might; and David was girded with a linen ephod. So David and all the house of Israel brought up the ark of the LORD with shouting, and with the sound of the trumpet. And as the ark of the LORD came into the city of David. Michal, Saul's daughter looked through a window, and saw king David leaping and dancing before the LORD: and she despised him in her heart"

David was leaping and dancing. He was not refined, but he knew how to dance and did it with all his might.

More than anything else, David was a product of grace. In 2 Samuel 12:13, the Bible says:

"And David said unto Nathan, I have sinned against the LORD. And Nathan said unto David, The LORD also hath put away thy sin; thou shalt not die."

Here was somebody who had just committed a series of very terrible sins. He committed adultery and fornication. As soon as Nathan told him what he had done. David repented and immediately, God forgave him, even though certain chastisements were to follow. If it were not for the grace of God, this would have been his end.

If we study what a Christian is supposed to be, we will find out that many of the things that we are to be, David was. There is a similarity between him and us. We too are kings and priests, according to Revelation 1:5-6:

> *"And from Jesus Christ, who is the faithful witness, and the first begotten of the dead, and the prince of the kings of the earth. Unto him that loved us, and washed us from our sins in his own blood, And hath made us kings and priests unto God and his Father: to him be glory and dominion for ever and ever."*

David was a warrior and we are also expected to be warriors. Ephesians 6:10-12 says:

> *"Finally, my brethren, be strong in the LORD, and in the power of his might. Put on the whole armour of God, that ye may be able to stand against the wiles of the devil. For we wrestle not against flesh and blood, but against principalities, against powers, against the rulers of the darkness of this world, against spiritual wickedness in high places."*

We are to be wrestlers. Our wrestle must however be against demons.

God expects every Christian to be a musician. Ephesians 5:19 says:

> *"Speaking to yourselves in psalms and hymns and spiritual songs, singing and making melody in your heart to the Lord:"*

God expects that even our conversation should be in song. We are to speak to one another in psalms, in hymns and in spiritual songs. The Bible tells us in 1 Peter 2:9 what kind of people we are:

> *"But ye are a chosen generation, a royal priesthood, an holy nation, a peculiar people: that ye should shew forth the praises of him who hath called you out of darkness into his marvellous light:"*

We are made priests and kings to praise God. We are supposed to compose music. We have a ten-string instrument to use – our ten fingers put together.

We are also supposed to be dancers. When you come before the Almighty God, one of the ways in which you are to praise Him is through dance. In Acts 2:16-17, the Bible says:

> *"But this is that which was spoken by the prophet Joel; And it shall come to pass in the last days, saith God, I will pour out my Spirit upon all flesh: and your sons and your daughters shall prophesy, and your young men shall see visions, and your old men shall dream dreams,"*

We are supposed to be prophets. God said He will pour His Spirit upon us and we will prophesy. In Ephesians 2:8, the Bible tells us that we also are saved by grace:

> *"For by grace are ye saved through faith; and that not of yourselves: it is the gift of God:"*

We are products of grace.

Chapter 2

BEWARE! GOD ALWAYS HAS A SUBSTITUTE

We will begin to study David in detail. The first mention of David is because God was angry with someone. God had appointed Saul as king. On the throne, he thought there was no one else that God could have made king but himself. God gave him instructions, but after a while, he started to go against them by doing what he liked. God then decided to set him aside and look for a substitute. 1 Samuel 16,and 13-14 says:

> "And the LORD said unto Samuel, How long wilt thou mourn for Saul, seeing I have rejected him from reigning over Israel? fill thine horn with oil, and go, I will send thee to Jesse the Bethlehemite: for I have provided me a king among his sons."

> "Then Samuel took the horn of oil, and anointed him in the midst of his brethren: and the spirit of the LORD came upon David from that day forward. So Samuel rose up, and went to Ramah. But the spirit of the LORD departed from Saul, and an evil spirit from the LORD troubled him."

One important thing we need to learn right away, from the life of David is that God always has a substitute. If God says He wants to use you, rejoice, but be careful, because even as He is choosing you He has already prepared a substitute. 1 Samuel 2:27-30 tells the sad story of Eli. God chose Eli and his family to serve Him. God changed His plans because He only honours those who honour Him. One thing about God is that He will not only replace you with someone else when He rejects you, but will also make sure that the devil takes you over. This was what happened with King Saul.

We also have the case of Judas Iscariot in Acts 1:16-20. He was a disciple of the Lord Jesus Christ. After betraying him, he ended up hanging himself. The Bible tells us something interesting in Psalm 75:6-7:

> *"For promotion cometh neither from the east, nor from the west, nor from the south. But God is the judge: he putteth down one, and setteth up another."*

Also Acts 10:34-35 says:

> *"Then Peter opened his mouth, and said, of a truth I perceive that God is no respecter of persons: But in every nation he that feareth him, and worketh righteousness, is accepted with him."*

I have seen many people who have been used of God who became too big for their boots, and God replaced them. Those ones that have been so replaced, though not dead yet, now live terrible lives. Whenever God gives you an opportunity to serve Him, humble yourself. It is better for God not to use you at all than to have used you and then push you aside. Once He pushes you aside, the devil takes over. I pray that God will never substitute you with somebody else. There is a warning in Revelation 3:11:

> *"Behold, I come quickly: hold that fast which thou hast, that no man take they crown."*

No one would have heard of David if King Saul had not lost his crown and position, just as nobody would have heard of Esther if Vashti had not lost her position. If Judas Iscariot had maintained his position, we never would have heard about Apostle Paul. God has given us these examples so that we can learn a lesson.

By the grace of God, I am going to hold fast to my salvation. Nobody is going to take my crown. I do not want God to replace me.

1 Samuel 16:1-10:

> *"And the LORD said unto Samuel, How long wilt thou mourn for Saul, seeing I have rejected him from reigning over Israel? Fill thine horn with oil, and go. I will send thee to Jesse the Bethlehemite: for I have provided me a king among his sons. And Samuel said, How can I go? If Saul hear it, he will kill me. And the LORD said, Take an heifer with thee, and say, I am come to sacrifice to the LORD. And call Jesse to the sacrifice, and I will shew thee what thou shalt do: and thou shalt anoint unto me him whom I name unto thee: And Samuel did that which the LORD spake, and came to Bethlehem. And the elders of the town trembled at his coming, and said, Comest thou peaceably? And he said, Peaceably: I am come to sacrifice unto the LORD: sanctify yourselves and come with me to the sacrifice. And he sanctified Jesse and his sons, and called them to the sacrifice. And it came to pass, when they were come, that he looked on Eliab, and said Surely the LORD's anointed is before him. But the LORD said unto Samuel, Look not on his countenance, or on the height of his stature; because I have refused him: for the LORD seeth not as a man seeth; for man looketh on the outward appearance, but the LORD looketh on the heart. Then Jesse called Abinadab, and made him pass before Samuel. And he said, Neither hath the LORD chosen this. Then Jesse made Shammah to pass by. And he said. Neither hath the LORD chosen this. Again, Jesse made seven of his sons to pass before Samuel. And Samuel said unto Jesse, The LORD hath not chosen these."*

God told Samuel to stop mourning over King Saul because He had already rejected him. He told Samuel to fill his oil and go and anoint one of the sons of Jesse as king. Samuel said Saul would kill him if he found out about his mission. This is an interesting statement because it shows clearly that Saul had degenerated so badly that he was considered capable of killing a servant of God. It is a terrible thing to backslide. This is why you must never touch sin. Once someone begins to slide backwards, there is no telling how far the fellow will go. When Samuel got to Bethlehem, the elders of the city trembled because a man of God had come on a visit. They trembled because they did not know whether he had come peacefully, or to pronounce God's judgement. We must take note here that whenever you see a man full of the Holy Spirit, do not handle him carelessly. The reason is simply that whatever he says is likely to happen. If he blesses you, you are surely blessed. If he should curse you, problems will come. The elders of the city trembled because of what is written in 1 Samuel 3:19:

> "And Samuel grew, and the LORD was with him, and did let none of his words fall to the ground."

His words came to pass by the power of God. This is why it is good for you to be in a position where your pastors can bless you.

Also, for the same reason, men of God should be careful not to get angry. If they become angry and say anything negative, it is likely to come to pass, and it may be difficult to reverse. If you are wise, you will not do anything that will make a man of God angry. The Bible is full of examples of instances where before a man of God who was filled with the Holy Spirit finished speaking, what they said came to pass. God said He would not let their words fall on the ground. We have the example of Elijah in 2 Kings 1:9-12, when a king sent some soldiers to arrest him. They wanted to arrest him. He said, if he be a man of God, let fire fall from Heaven to consume the soldiers. Before he finished speaking, fire fell.

There is also the example of Elisha, in 2 Kings 2:19-22. Here Elisha said the water of Jericho was now safe to drink and so it was, according to the words of Elisha. Elisha blessed the water that day and the blessing came to pass. Immediately after this, some children confronted Elisha and they began to mock him (2 Kings 2:23-24). Elisha turned and cursed the children. Before he finished speaking, two she-bears came out from the bush and tore forty-two of the children into pieces. In Joshua 6:26, Joshua pronounced a curse on Jericho. He said anyone who tries to rebuild the wall of Jericho would lose his first son while laying the foundation and his last son will die when finishing it. If you read 1 Kings 16:34, you will find that after many years, a man started to rebuild Jericho. His first son died the day he laid the foundation and the day be completed the job, his last son died.

There is also the account in Joshua 10:12-13. When Joshua spoke to the sun and moon to stand still. As soon as he spoke, everything stood still because it was the Holy Spirit that was speaking through him. We also have the example of our Lord Jess Christ in Mark 11:12-14. Jesus saw a fig tree, and expected to find fruit on it, but He found nothing. He then cursed the tree. He said no man would eat from it again. The following morning, in Mark 11:20-23, the disciples saw that the fig tree had dried up from the roots. It is terrible thing to be cursed by a man of God. You may not know the impact immediately but it will come later. When Jesus cursed the fig tree, nothing happened to it immediately but it soon died. Anyone of us filled with the Holy Spirit can speak and it will come to pass. This is why I always counsel parents never to say anything negative to their children. I always keep on saying to myself that my tomorrow will be alright. By saying this, I am decreeing, for I am saying it with the backing of the Holy Spirit, so it will come to pass. Why not prophesy to yourself, right away?

We find another good example in Acts 13:6-12. Paul was preaching the Gospel and a sorcerer tried to hinder him. He told to him he would go blind for a season. The man became blind immediately.

Going back to Samuel's visit to Bethlehem, after the elders of the city trembled, Samuel told them not to worry because he came to sacrifice to God. He then told them to sanctify themselves and join him in the sacrifice. In those days, when you wanted to worship God, you had to sanctify yourself first. You had to set yourself apart. If you want to serve God acceptably now, you have to be holy. You cannot avoid it. If you come to the house of God to praise Him, sing and give your offerings and you are not holy, you are wasting your efforts. Romans 12:1-2 says:

> *"I beseech you therefore, brethren, by the mercies of God, that ye Present your bodies a living sacrifice, holy, acceptable unto God, which is your reasonable service. And be not conformed to this world: but be ye transformed by the renewing of your mind, that ye may prove what is that good, and acceptable, and perfect, will of God."*

To worship God, you must first be holy. According to John 4:23-24, God is Spirit and those who worship Him must worship Him in spirit and in truth. What kind of Spirit is God? We know that God is a Holy Spirit. If you are going to worship Him, you must worship in holiness of spirit. This is why he said in 1 Peter 1:15-16:

"But as he which hath called you is holy, so be ye holy in all manner of conversation; Because it is written, be ye holy; for I am holy."

Any time you enter the house of God, go in sanctified, and as you are supposed to be in the house of God regularly, this means you must be sanctified regularly. Furthermore, your body is the temple of God because the Holy Spirit is within you. This is why you have to be holy continually.

When Samuel arrived in Bethlehem, he called Jesse and his sons to the sacrifice. When Jesse started bringing out his sons, Eliab came out first. He was a tall, impressive man and when Samuel saw him, he thought this must be the chosen one. God told him that he had already rejected Eliab. He said man looks on the surface while God looks at the heart. In Isaiah 55:8, God says:

"For my thoughts are not your thoughts, neither are your ways my ways, saith the LORD."

Man looks at the outside while God sees the inside. In 1 Samuel 2:3, the Bible says:

"Talk no more so exceeding proudly: let not arrogancy come out of your mouth: for the LORD is a God of knowledge, and by him actions are weighed."

Everything you do is being weighed by God to find out why you are doing it. He will want to know the motive behind everything you are doing. Are you doing things to attract the attention of your pastor? Or to impress the person next to you? Why do you come to church? Is it to impress the pastor or your friends? Or are you coming because you love God? He weighs our actions. You cannot hide from God. There is a lesson for young people here. Proverbs 31:30 says:

"Favour is deceitful, and beauty is vain: but a woman that feareth the LORD, she shall be praised."

If you marry a girl because she is beautiful, you may be marrying a demon. If you marry a man because he is handsome, you may be marrying a fallen angel. Beauty can deceive. God says it is the one who fears the Lord that should be praised. God said He had rejected Eliab. I pray that God will never reject you.

We need to study the lives of the people that God rejected in the Bible so that we can learn some lessons from their history. We have to know what God saw in their lives to make Him reject them so that we can avoid making their mistakes.

Our first example is in Genesis 4:3-7 where Cain was rejected because he brought an unacceptable sacrifice. God asked for a sacrifice of an animal – in other words, a blood sacrifice Cain gave a sacrifice of fruit and grain. God rejected his sacrifice. I have heard people say that whatever you put in an envelope and label 'tithe' is your tithe. They do this as if God does not understand mathematics and cannot calculate. This is why some people find that their sacrifices are rejected constantly. Another person who was rejected was Esau. Why was Esau rejected? The Bible tells us in Hebrews 12:15-17:

> *"Looking diligently lest any man fail of the grace of God; lest any root of bitterness springing up trouble you, and thereby many be defiled; Lest there be any fornicator, or profane person, as Esau, who for one morsel of meat sold his birthright. For ye know how that afterward, when he would have inherited the blessing, he was rejected: for he found no place of repentance, though he sought it carefully with tears."*

He was rejected because he could not control his appetite. I pray that your stomach will not send you to hell. Some people have never fasted since they became Christians. I pray that your appetite would be brought under control.

Another example is the tribe of Ephraim. God gave them the blessing that would have gone to the tribe of Manasseh. After they prospered, they forgot God. They joined themselves with idols. God said in Hosea 4:17:

> *"Ephraim is joined to idols: let him alone."*

Later in Hosea 5:9, God said:

> *"Ephraim shall be desolate in the day of rebuke: among the tribes of Israel have I made known that which shall surely be."*

When God rejects a man, his destruction will follow imminently. The common fault in almost all the people rejected by God is pride. We have a classic example in the story of Vashti, in Esther 1:10-19. The King sent for his queen,

Vashti, to come and show her beauty to his guests during a banquet. Vashti said she would not come. What happened next was that Vashti was deposed as queen forthwith. You are whatever you are by the grace of God. He is the One who made you. His is the One who promoted you. It is God who is keeping you alive. If He takes His breath from you, even for just a minute, you will soon discover that you are mere dust. Nothing destroys a man faster than pride. The Bible had a lot to say about pride. For example, Psalm 138:6 says:

> *"Though the LORD be high, yet hath he respect unto the lowly: but proud he knoweth afar off."*

The Most High God says the only people He respects are the humble and lowly person. He says He hates the proud. Again, in James 4:6 the Bible says:

> *"But he giveth more. Wherefore he said, God resisteth the proud, but giveth grace unto the humble."*

God resists the proud. There is no room for pride in the vicinity of God. In Matthew 23:10-12, the Bible says:

> *"Neither be ye called masters: for one is your Master, even Christ. But he that is greatest among you shall be your servant. And whosoever shall exalt himself shall be abased: and he that shall humble himself shall be exalted."*

God said he had rejected Eliab. Pray that God will not reject you. Ask Him to reveal any areas of pride in your life so that you can do something about them. I do not want God to reject me.

Chapter 3

THE LORD'S DECISION IS ALWAYS FINAL

1 Samuel 16:11-12

> *"And Samuel said unto Jesse, Are here all thy children? And he said, There remaineth yet the youngest, and behold, he keepeth the sheep. And Samuel said unto Jesse, Send and fetch him: for we will not sit down till he come hither. And he sent, and brought him in. Now he was ruddy, and withal of a beautiful countenance, and goodly to look to. And the LORD said, Arise, anoint him: for this is he."*

Samuel had told Jesse to bring all the members of his family to the sacrifice but Jesse ignored David. He did not bother to send for him out in the fields. He decided that if God was going to anoint a king out of his children, it could not be the last born. He made up his mind that it would be the one who was only fit to look after the sheep. When it was time to present his children, he started with the firstborn, Eliab. God rejected him. He presented the next six and God rejected them all. Jesse did not tell the man of God that he had one son left. It was the man of God who asked if he had any other son left, knowing full well that he had heard correctly from God. It was after the question that he said, reluctantly, that there was one more son, who was looking after the sheep. It was the response of Jesse that made Samuel insist that they would not sit down until David arrived.

David was looking after the sheep and singing praises to God. As a shepherd, he had plenty of time to worship God. He was there worshipping when he was sent for and told that there was a man of God who said nobody would sit down until he returned home. David must have been wondering if he was to become the servant of the prophet. However, when he arrived, he discovered that God had chosen him to be king.

GOD IS NOT A DEMOCRAT

The first thing we note here immediately is that God is not a democrat. If it were decided by vote, David would never have become king. If it were by vote, many of us would not have been saved. If God had called our friends together and asked them to do a secret ballot to find out whether we should be healed, many of us would not be healed.

God does not ask anybody whether He should save us or not. He just goes ahead and saves our souls. He does not ask anybody whether He should heal you. He just goes ahead and heals you.

God is an absolute monarch. In Genesis 1:1-4, when the whole earth was full of darkness and everything was empty, He said 'Let there be light', and there was light and not darkness. He did not say that there should be a vote whether to have darkness or light. He merely decreed. I pray that He would dictate light into your life, in the Name of Jesus Christ. Psalm 115:3, the Bible says:

"But our God is in the heavens: he hath done whatsoever he hath pleased."

God is Almighty. He just decides what he wants to do and does it. In Psalm 33:11:

"The counsel of the Lord standeth forever, the thoughts of his heart to all generations."

Once He has decided on something, it is a settled matter. In Psalm 33:8-9, the Bible says:

> *"Let all the earth fear the LORD: let all the inhabitants of the world stand in awe of him. For he spake, and it was done: he commanded, and it stood fast."*

Job 33:13 says:

> *"Why doest thou strive against him? for he giveth not account of any of his matters."*

The decision of the Lord is always final. Once He has made up His mind about something, nothing can change it. All this should be good news to us because in Jeremiah 29:11, the Bible says that God has some good thoughts concerning us. His plan for our lives is a good one. His counsel shall stand. Whether the devil liked it or not. He had decided, even before David was born, that he would become a king.

He had decided, even before you were born, that you would be saved. This is why you are saved. It is His final decision that it will be well with you. He told Jeremiah in Jeremiah 1:4-5:

> *"Then the word of the Lord came unto me, saying, Before I formed thee in the belly I knew thee; and before thou comest forth out of the womb I sanctified thee, and I ordained thee a prophet unto the nations"*

Before you were born, God knew it would be well with you. This is why you believed the gospel. Many hear the gospel and reject it. God has a plan for your life and you should really praise Him for this. God had mapped out the life of Saul of Tarsus, as he wrote in Galatians 1:15-16. He said he persecuted the church of God but when the time came, the God who had separated him from his mother's womb revealed His grace in Him:

> *"But when it pleased God, who separated me from my mother's womb, and called me by his grace, To reveal his Son in me, that I might preach him among the heathen; immediately I conferred not with flesh and blood:"*

Each time I think of the sovereignty of God – the prerogative of God to decide what to do – it frightens me. When you read Romans 9:17 which says God created Pharaoh for destruction, you are bound to be frightened. He was made to become a great king so as to be drowned in the Red Sea, that generations to come would acknowledge the greatness of God. I thank God that He did not make me like Pharaoh. Whenever you read Job 21:29-30, you will always thank God for the salvation of your soul:

> *"Have ye not asked them that go by the way? And do ye not know their tokens, That the wicked is reserved to the day of destruction? They shall be brought forth to the day of wrath."*

The wicked are reserved for the day of destruction. Sinners are reserved for the day of destruction. Whenever I considered that there was a time that I would have been described as a wicked man, I always thank God that now I am reserved for the glory of God. Likewise, if I reflect on what He said in Romans 9:15-16:

> *"For He saith to Moses, I will have mercy on whom I will have mercy, and I will have compassion on whom I will have compassion. So then it is not of him that willeth, nor of him that runneth, but of God that showeth mercy."*

I thank God that He showed mercy on me.

WHEN YOUR DAY COMES, NOTHING CAN HINDER YOU

The day of David came while he was in the hills, looking after the sheep. David never dreamt that he could become a king. There was no king in his family and in any case, King Saul was still alive and well. David was not the son of King Saul so it could not have crossed his mind that he would ever become king. He never prayed for it.

Often, we pray for certain miracles, not knowing that God has reserved something even better for us. The Bible says God can do exceedingly more abundantly than we can ask or think. Before you were born, the Almighty God had written the blueprint of your life.

In 1 Samuel 9:1-21, we are first introduced to Saul. His father lost some asses and Saul was told to go with a servant to look for them. He looked for asses and he received a kingdom. After looking for three days, he decided to go home so that his father would not be worried about him. On his way, he decided to enquire of the whereabouts of the asses from a man of God. As they were going to the house of the man of God, God was already speaking to the man of God that someone was coming to him and that he was going to be the new king.

Likewise, the first mention of Elisha, in 1 Kings 19:19-21, we find him busy working on the farm when the Almighty God tells him that his day had come. He became the son of a prophet. In the story of Gideon in Judges 6:11-16, the Bible tells us that Gideon was threshing wheat near the winepress, and the Almighty God met him there. You may be working in a factory and God may meet you there. When your day comes, nothing can stop it. We are told in Exodus 3:1-10, that Moses was living in the desert where you wouldn't even think of looking to find a deliverer. You may live in a village that is not even on the map but God can pick you up from there. You may be a servant like Joshua, the servant of Moses who was in a tent, in deep sorrow, because his master had just died. God met him there and said he was to succeed Moses. Joshua trembled but God said He would be with him just as He was with Moses.

You may be familiar with the story of Joseph in Genesis 41:8-14. Joseph was in prison and had been forgotten. He was sentenced for an offence that he did not even commit. There were two servants of Pharaoh with him in the prison that dreamed dreams and Joseph correctly interpreted them. He told the one who had the good dream to remember him when he was restored to Pharaoh's service. When the servant got out, he forgot Joseph. When the day of Joseph came, God sent two vivid dreams to Pharaoh. After those dreams, Pharaoh could not sleep and he brought all the wise men in the land together, but they could not interpret the dreams.

It was then that the servant remembered Joseph. He had forgotten simply because the day of Joseph had not come. When his day came, God arranged everything. When the Almighty God wants to do something, He does not need your help. He will do everything in His own way. When your day comes, even if you are in prison, God will lift you up. Your moment can come inside the church as in the case of Zacharias in Luke 1:5-20. He was there ministering to God and an angel appeared to him. For years, he had longed for a child. He had lost hope. However, God had His plans and a timetable: Right inside the

Temple, his day came. In Luke 1:26-38 we have the story of Mary, a young virgin who was minding her own business. She was certainly not expecting that God would tell her she had been chosen to be the mother of His Child. An angel appears to her and told her that it was her day. From that day on, Mary was never the same again.

David woke up a shepherd boy and by the time he went to bed, he was a king. Today may be your day. It may be the day that you will receive all the gifts of the Holy Spirit. It may be the day that you will be given answers to all your prayers. All that you need to do is to worship God and allow your destiny to be fulfilled. You must remember, however, that the day came for Gehazi too. He was a servant of a man of God, but, and he was a very crooked one. God was watching him, and one day, his day came. He ran after Naaman to get something good. Instead he got leprosy.

Do not let today be your day of destruction. If you are still in sin, let today be your day of salvation.

Chapter 4

———◆◆◆———

WHAT KIND OF PERSON WILL GOD CHOOSE?

1 Samuel 16:12:

> *"And he sent, and brought him in. Now he was ruddy, and withal of a beautiful countenance, and goodly to look to. And the LORD said, Arise, anoint him: for this is he."*

When they brought in David, the first thing that God said to the man of God was that he was the chosen one. The Almighty God said that David was His choice. What kind of people does God choose? 1 Corinthians 1:26-29 gives us a clue:

> *"For ye see your calling, brethren, how that not many wise men after the flesh, not many mighty, not many noble, are called: But God hath chosen the weak things of the world to confound the things which are mighty; And base things of the world, and things which are despised, hath God chosen, yea, and things which are not, to bring to nought things that are: That no flesh should glory in his presence."*

God will choose the foolish. God will choose the weak. God will choose the people that are regarded as nothing. Why will God choose the foolish? Because

He can fill them with His wisdom. If you believe you are already wise, He can no longer fill you with wisdom so He will not use you. This is probably why we find very few intellectuals in the service of God. By the time God is telling them to go to the right, they will tell Him a hundred reasons why they should go to the left. A foolish man is likely to do whatever God says. If he needs wisdom for anything at all, he will ask God and God will give it to him. The Bible says in James 1:5-6:

"If any of you lack wisdom, let him ask of God, that giveth to all men liberally, and upbraideth not; and it shall be given him. But let him ask in faith, nothing wavering. For he that wavereth is like a wave of the sea driven with the wind and tossed."

Many things that God does do not conform to human logic. For example, God says if you want to be rich, you must give. God says if you want your home to overflow with blessings, you must pay all your tithes. This does not seem logical. For some people, the full 100% of their earnings are not sufficient, so how can they manage on 90%? When I became a Christian, I really argued with God about tithing. I thank God that He took my wisdom from me and replaced it with His foolishness and that is why I am where I am today. The first time that I paid my tithes was on Sunday and the following Monday, I was blessed financially with an academic grant that I did not even know existed. You cannot dictate to God how He will bless you. He has the blessings reserved. Follow His so-called foolish ways and you will see that the foolishness of God is wiser than the wisdom of man.

Why will God choose weak people? He will choose weak people so that He can fill them with His power. If you are already strong, how can God give you strength? Isaiah 40:29-31 says:

"He giveth power to the faint; and to them that have no might he increaseth strength. Even the youths shall faint and be weary, and the young men shall utterly fall: But they that wait upon the LORD shall renew their strength; they shall mount up with wings as eagles; they shall run, and not be weary; and they shall walk, and not faint."

If you say that your strength is the strength of youth, a time will come when you will exhaust the energy in you. Nevertheless, if you wait upon the Lord, you will constantly have your strength renewed by God. Before I became a Christian, I was a sportsman but malaria often laid me low, at least once a month. After I was converted, I discussed the matter with the Lord. I told Him to heal me and I would serve Him. He healed me and I am now serving Him. I work more than ten times harder than I used to work ten years ago but by the grace of God, I am stronger now than I was then. The secret is that they that wait upon the Lord shall renew their strength. There are some strong people who do not ask for the support of God and they run out of energy. There also are those who are weak who rely solely on God and His energy flows through them.

Why does God choose those who are nothing? It is because, if you are already something, it becomes difficult for God to use you. One feature of God is that He begins to lift people up little by little to make them something. 1 Samuel 2:8 says:

> *"He raiseth up the poor out of the dust, and lifteth up the beggar from the dunghill, to set them among princes, and to make them inherit the throne of glory: for the pillars of the earth are the LORD's and he hath set the world upon them."*

You may be saying you are already wise, strong and someone important, but yet you want God to use you. If you want Him to use you, you will have to reduce yourself to nothing. You have to set aside your wisdom. You have to forget your strength. You have to forget that you are somebody. If you do not do these things, He will never use you. If you are ever to be used by God, you must be able to say like John the Baptist in John 3:30:

"He must increase, but I must decrease."

The moment you decide that you want God to use you, you have to forget your education, your strength and your position, and reduce yourself to nothing so that God can pick you up and make you become something. There is no other way. Those that God will choose must be the foolish, the weak and the nobodies of this world so that He can give them His wisdom, His strength and His glory. Ultimately, whatever God may achieve through them, they will not take any glory for it because they know that whatever happened was from God. John humbled himself, but Jesus Christ said that of all men born of women, there was none greater than John the Baptist. God saw John as His representative. The representatives of God are those who do everything in His Name. They are the ambassadors of God. They are those who go to represent Him. They are those who go ahead to announce that Jesus Christ is coming. Luke 10:1 and 17 says:

"After these things the Lord appointed other seventy also, and sent them two and two before his face into every city and place, whither he himself would come."

"And the seventy returned again with joy, saying, Lord, even the devils are subject unto us through they name."

David is a classic example of a representative of God, as we find in 1 Samuel 17:45:

"Then said David to the Philistine, Thou comest to me with a sword, and with a spear, and with a shield: but I come to thee in the name of the LORD of hosts, the God of the armies of Israel, whom thou hast defiled."

David said he was there in the name of the Lord of hosts. He told the Philistine not to look at him but to look at the One who sent him. A representative of the Almighty God will always be victorious. The Bible tells us that you too can be His representative, in Mark 16:17-18, we read:

"And these signs shall follow them that believe; In my name shall they cast out devils; they shall speak with new tongues; They shall take up serpents; and if they drink any deadly thing, it shall not hurt them; they shall lay hands on the sick, and they shall recover."

God said David was His choice. It means that David was chosen to be His spokesman. You too can be God's spokesman.

In Exodus 4:10-12, Moses was not sure that he was up to the job of being God's spokesman:

"And Moses said unto the LORD, O my Lord, I am not eloquent, neither

heretofore, nor since thou hast spoken unto they servant: but I am slow of speech, and of a slow tongue. And the LORD said unto him, Who hath made man's mouth? or who maketh the dumb, or deaf, or the seeing, or the blind? have not I the Lord? Now therefore go, and I will be with thy mouth, and teach thee what thou shalt say."

Here we see again classical example of those that God will use. God wanted to choose a spokesman and He chose someone who stammers. One thing about the spokesman of God is that they do not speak unless God gives them something to say. David said in Psalm 51:15:

"O Lord, open thou my lips; and my mouth shall shew forth they praise."

David was saying here that if God does not open his lips, his mouth will remain shut. A talkative person is unlikely to become a spokesman of God. God will more likely choose a dumb person.

To become a spokesman of God, you must be ready to surrender your tongue to God. This is why you speak in new tongues when you are baptised in the Holy Spirit. Speaking in new tongues means that you have surrendered your tongue to the Holy Spirit. You will then become a witness of Jesus Christ.

God then said David should be anointed. This implies several things. It means he was to be set apart for God. It also means he was to be empowered. We have several similar examples of this in the Bible. God separated Paul and Barnabas for His use. There were many men of God in the meeting but out of the whole gathering, God chose only two people. When God separates someone by anointing, He means that this person is His own and should be touched by nobody. In Psalm 105:14-15, we are told:

"Touch not mine anointed, and do my prophets no harm."

In 1 Samuel 24:2-6 when King Saul was pursuing David to kill him, there came a day when David had the opportunity to kill Saul, but did not. He was aware that King Saul was still the anointed of God, even though he had lost favour with God. Even though David himself was anointed, he dared not strike another anointed man of God. The judgement of the anointed is in the hands of God so if you see such a person doing anything wrong, pray for him instead of going against them.

In Jude 9, the Bible tells us that even Archangel Michael could not say any contrary word to Satan when he had a confrontation with him. This is because he recognised that Satan was an anointed cherub. Michael left judgement in God's hands. However, we are children of God, and therefore have the right to resist the devil. Jesus Christ gave this right to us.

In Jeremiah 2:2-3, the Bible makes it clear to us that the anointed must remain holy unto the Lord if he or she is to retain the privileges of an anointed person:

> *"Go and cry in the ears of Jerusalem, saying, Thus saith the LORD: I remember thee, the kindness of thy youth, the love of thine espousals, when thou wentest after me in the wilderness, in a land that was not sown. Israel was holiness unto the LORD, and the firstfruits of his increase: all that devour him shall offend: evil shall come upon them, saith the LORD."*

When Israel was holy, anyone who came against them would suffer. To anoint David also means to empower him. Any time that God chooses someone and makes them His representative, He will equip them. In Matthew 10:1, the Bible says:

> *"And when he had called unto him twelve disciples, he gave them power against unclean spirits, to cast them out, and to heal all manner of disease."*

The representatives of God are always given the power of God. This is why Jesus Christ told His disciples in Luke 24-49 to tarry in Jerusalem until they received power from above. Even Jesus Christ had to wait to be anointed with the Holy Spirit and power before He began to do His works (Acts 10:38). If you are called to be God's representative you must receive power. This will happen when the Holy Ghost comes upon you, so if you want to be God's choice, go ahead and ask Him to anoint you.

Chapter 5

———————◆◆◆◆———————

GOD OR DEMON?

1 Samuel 16:13-14:

> "Then Samuel took the horn of oil, and anointed him in the midst of his brethren: and the Spirit of the LORD came upon David from that day forward. So Samuel rose up, and went to Ramah. But the Spirit of the LORD departed from Saul, and an evil spirit from the LORD troubled him."

As soon as Samuel anointed David, the Spirit of the Lord came on him. When the Holy Spirit came on David, He simultaneously departed from Saul and demons took over. There are several implications here. However, one thing we have to note immediately is that it is possible for human beings to become the house of God. 1 Corinthians 6:19 calls us the temples of the Holy Spirit:

> "What? Know ye not that your body is the temple of the Holy Ghost which is in you, which ye have of God, and ye are not your own?"

You can be the temple inside which the Holy Spirit will live, so your home can also become the house of God, if for instance, you host a house group.

From time to time, we find Paul writing to someone and telling the person to greet the church in his house. If there is a church in your house, you can be sure that Almighty God will be there. He says where two or three people are gathered in His name, He will be there. Wherever God is, there will be light there. Where light is to be found, darkness cannot stay. According to Acts 2:37-39, if you repent of your sins and you are baptised by immersion, it becomes possible for you to be filled with the Holy Spirit. Peter said that the promise is for us and our children. It is for all whom the Lord will call:

> *"Now when they heard this, they were pricked in their heart, and said unto Peter and to the rest of the apostles, Men and brethren, what shall we do? Then Peter said unto them, Repent, and be baptized everyone of you in the name of Jesus Christ for the remission of sins, and ye shall receive the gift of the Holy Ghost. For the promise is unto you, and to your children, and to all that are afar off, even as many as the Lord our God shall call."*

I believe that God is ready to live in anyone who is willing to open up to Him. Once the Holy Spirit moves in, certain things will begin to happen. When God is dwelling in your heart, you can be sure that He will not come empty handed. As a matter of fact, in 1 Corinthians 12:4-11, the Bible lists at least nine gifts that the Holy Spirit will bring when He comes to dwell in us. These gifts can be classified into three groups.

(i) The Revelatory Gifts
    a) The word of wisdom
    b) The word of knowledge
    c) The discerning of spirits
ii) The Gifts of Inspiration:
    a) Prophecy
    b) Speaking in tongues
    c) Interpretation of tongues
iii) The Gifts of Power:
    a) Faith.
    b) Healing.
    c) Working of Miracles.

When you have these gifts available to you all the time, you will find out that it becomes easy for you to win souls. In Acts 2:41, Peter preached one sermon and he won 3,000 souls. I am sure that there are many Christians who would be extremely happy if they are able to win 3,000 converts in one year. By the time Peter preached his second sermon, in Acts 4:4, 5,000 souls were saved.

Once the Holy Ghost begins to dwell in you, everyone you touch will receive healing, according to Acts 3:1-8. This is the account of the lame man by the Beautiful Gate. John and Peter had seen him there for long time but they could not help him. In Acts 2, Peter received the baptism in the Holy Spirit and in Acts 3, he grabbed the man and he saw the power of the Holy Spirit in action. If the Holy Spirit is dwelling in you, even the sweat coming out of you will be anointed. This is what the Bible tells us in Acts 19:11-12, about Paul:

> *"And God wrought special miracles by the hands of Paul: So that from his body were brought unto the sick handkerchiefs or aprons, and the diseases departed from them, and the evil spirits went out of them."*

Your sweat can contain power if you allow the Holy Spirit to fill you, in fact, even your shadows can heal, as Peter's shadow did in Acts 5:14-16:

> *"And believers were the more added to the Lord, multitudes both of men and women. Insomuch that they brought forth the sick into the streets, and laid them on beds and couches, that at the least the shadow of Peter passing by might overshadow some of them. There came also a multitude out of the cities round about unto Jerusalem, bringing sick folks, and them which were vexed with unclean spirits: and they were healed everyone."*

With this kind of power, you will be able to tear into pieces every spiritual lion, witch and wizard that wants to attack you, just like Samson in Judges 14:5-6. The Bible tells us that as Samson was passing by, a young lion roared at him. He was filled with the Holy Spirit and tore the lion into two. One person filled with the Holy Spirit can face a thousand enemies as we see in Judges 15:14-15, when Samson was brought to Lehi and the Philistines thought they had finally captured him. The Bible tells us that the Holy Spirit came mightily upon him and all the cords binding him became loose. He found the jawbone of an ass and before they could flee, he killed 1,000 of them. When the power of God comes upon you, any enemy that is wise will run. Those who stay will perish.

Later on, in Judges 14:2-3, when the Philistines found out that Samson was in Gaza they surrounded the city and shut the gate. They then decided to wait until morning before attacking him so that there would be plenty of light to flee by, if they needed so to do. At midnight, Samson got up, shook the gate and uprooted it. When you become full of the Holy Spirit, you will be able to move huge obstacles. You also achieve more through prayers prayed at midnight than at other times.

When you are full of the Holy Spirit, it becomes easy for you to live a holy life. There will be no struggle and you will just discover that holiness is as easy as breathing. The Holy Spirit will then begin to produce fruits in you. When you are full of the Holy Spirit, people will begin to discover certain new things happening in your life. Look at Galatians 5:22-23:

> *"But the fruit of the Spirit is love, joy, longsuffering, gentleness, goodness, faith, Meekness, temperance: against such there is no law."*

How would you like it if God were to write a testimony about you saying that you were full of love, joy, peace, gentleness, longsuffering and full of faith? If God is able to write about you like this you can be sure that Heaven will be your home.

Whenever the Holy Spirit is dwelling in you, he will be the One producing the fruit. You will just find out that all the things that used to annoy you do not annoy you anymore. In the past, I used to be often annoyed with people but when the Holy Spirit filled me, it suddenly began to occur to me that God did not make all people the same. I began to see that people behave according to the ability and brain that God has given them. Now instead of being angry with them, I become compassionate.

When you are full of the Holy Spirit, you suddenly become gentle, longsuffering, kind and good. People will see you and say you are very much like Christ. It is the Holy Spirit in you that is bringing forth the fruit. However, the choice is still yours. You are still free to welcome spirits. Ephesians 5:18 says:

> *"And be not drunk with wine, wherein is excess; but be filled with the Spirit."*

Another word for hot drink is "spirits". When you are drinking alcohol, you are imbibing spirits. The Bible admonishes us not to take these spirits but to be filled with the Holy Spirit. The human body has tremendous capacity either for God or for the devil. A man can house as many demons as are allowed inside. Mary Magdalene had only seven demons. In Luke 8:26-30, we encounter a man that had as many as a legion of demons. A legion means at least 1,000. One single individual can be possessed by at least 1,000 demons at a time.

We find that the words of Jesus are still true today. He said in Joshua 24:15:

> *"And if it seem evil unto you to serve the LORD, choose you this day whom ye will serve; whether the gods which your fathers served that were on the other side of the flood, or the gods of the Amorites, in whose land ye dwell: but as for me and my house, we will serve the LORD:"*

You can allow an evil spirit to fill you as it filled Ananias and Sapphira in Acts 5:1-5. On the other hand, like Paul in Acts 13:6-12, you can allow yourself to be filled with the `Holy Spirit, and you will begin to see the glory of God even while you are still here on earth. With time, God will allow you a glimpse of what is waiting for you in Heaven.

IT IS DANGEROUS TO BE DISCARDED BY GOD.

When the Spirit of God left King Saul, evil spirits came to trouble him. When God discards someone, He will make sure that something happens to them in order that others may learn a few lessons. It is far better never to have been used by God than to be discarded. When Eli was discarded, in 1 Samuel 4:10-22, his two sons died on the same day. He died too and his daughter-in-law died during childbirth. The child was named Ichabod which means, 'the glory has departed'. When Vashti was discarded in Esther 1:19-21, it was decreed that she must be banished. In the morning she was a queen but by evening, she was not just an ordinary woman but was banned from coming before the king.

If you read Matthew 10:1, you will discover that Judas Iscariot once cast out demons. Later, we read in Matthew 27:3-5, that he hung himself. This is why Paul said in 1 Corinthians 9:27 that he kept his body in subjection so that after his race, he would not become a castaway. Once God discards you, the devil will take over. There is no room in nature for a vacuum. Either you are full of the Holy Spirit or you are full of demons.

If you have not yet believed on Jesus, you are walking on dangerous ground because if you are not for God, you are for the devil. You have to take a stand. If you are a backslider, I advise you to run quickly back to God before demons fill you. If you are already a Christian, ask God to fill you to overflow with the Holy Spirit.

Chapter 6

MUSIC AND DELIVERANCE

1 Samuel 16:14-23:

"But the Spirit of the LORD departed from Saul, and an evil spirit from the LORD troubled him. And Saul's servants said unto him, Behold now; an evil spirit from God troubleth thee. Let our lord now command thy servants, which are before thee, to seek out a man, who is a cunning player on an harp; and it shall come to pass, when the evil spirit from God is upon thee, that he shall play with his hand, and thou shalt be well. And Saul said unto his servants, Provide me now a man that can play well, and bring him to me. Then answered one of the servants, and said, Behold, I have seen a son of Jesse the Bethlehemite, that is cunning in playing, and a mighty valiant man, and a man of war, and prudent in matters, and a comely person, and the LORD is with him. Wherefore Saul sent messengers unto Jesse, and said, send me David they son, which is with the sheep. And Jesse took an ass laden with bread, and a bottle of wine, and a kid, and sent them by David his son unto Saul. And David came to Saul, and stood before him: and he loved him greatly; and he became his armourbearer. And Saul sent to Jesse, saying, Let David, I pray thee, stand before me; for he hath found favour in

my sight. And it came to pass, when the evil spirit from God was upon Saul, that David took an harp, and played with his hand: so Saul was refreshed, and was well, and the evil spirit departed from him. "

There are many things to take note in the above passage but we will concentrate on verse 23. However, before then, we should note in passing that when the evil spirit came on King Saul, it was evident to his servants. People will know if somebody is being controlled by the devil. In the same manner, you cannot hide it when the Holy Spirit is controlling your life. A city that is set upon the hill cannot be hidden.

THE ROLE OF MUSIC IN DELIVERANCE

Spiritual music drives away demons. As you are playing spiritual music, praising and glorifying God, demons, who are the enemies of God, will become uncomfortable. No one wants to stay where his enemies are being praised. If the demons can stop you, they will try. If they cannot stop you, they will leave. This is why we must be careful what kind of songs we sing. There are some songs that sound beautiful but they do not really praise God.

Just as spiritual music drives demons away, worldly music invites demons in. Hence, demons have infiltrated the music in many churches today, so that when they are singing to praise God, you can barely tell the difference between what they are singing and reggae music. Most of the worldly music is the kind of music they sing in Hell. When somebody is in pain, he is likely to make a sound similar to that of worldly music. This is why we must go back to the way we used to praise Him.

Also, divine music invites the Holy Spirit. In 2 Kings 3:13-15, the Bible records that several kings came to Elisha asking him to give them a word of prophecy. He was angry because one of the kings was an idol worshipper and he told the king to go and consult his idol. Because he was angry, the Holy Spirit being a gentle dove, moved away from Elisha. To call the Holy Spirit back, he had to ask for a minstrel who played the kind of music that God wants to hear. The Bible says as the minstrel was playing, the hand of God was on Elisha. The Holy Spirit came back and he was able to prophesy.

In Psalm 22:3, the Bible tells us that God inhabits the praises of His people. When people are praising Him and magnifying His holy Name, the Almighty God draws near. When God draws near. He does not walk alone. Wherever, God goes, the hosts of Heaven will follow Him. In Acts 16:25 Paul and Silas were in prison, bound. At midnight they prayed and sang praises to God. All the prisoners heard them.

White they were praising God. He arose and drew close to those who were praising Him. The host of Heaven followed Him and their movement caused an earthquake, which loosened all the prisoners' chains. This implies that when they were praising God, deliverance came. There was also spiritual deliverance for the Jailer and his household.

If you want to invite God to come into your situation, you should begin to praise Him. If He will come to where you are, He must first arise from His throne Psalm 68:1-4 tells us what happens when God arises.

"Let God arise, let his enemies be scattered: let them also that hate him flee before him. As smoke is driven away, so drive them away, as wax melteth before the fire, so let the wicked perish at the presence of God. But let the righteous be glad, let them rejoice before God: yea, let them exceedingly rejoice. Sing unto God, sing praises to his name: extol him that rideth upon the heavens by his name JAH, and rejoice before him."

When God arises, His enemies will be scattered. When a child of God is in bondage and it is not God keeping him there, when he begins to praise God, God will arise and His enemies will be scattered so that and the child of God will be freed. David says in Psalm 18:1-3

"I will love thee, O Lord, my strength. The LORD is my rock, and my fortress, and my deliverer; my God, my strength, in whom I will trust; my buckler, and the horn of my salvation, and my high tower. I will call upon the LORD, who is worthy to be praised: so shall I be saved from mine enemies."

David is saying here that God is worthy to be praised. Here he calls God certain names to praise Him. He said that this is how he will call upon the Lord and be saved from his enemies. David knew how to be set free from the enemy. He had many enemies who pursued him for several years but God delivered him from them all. God is a loving Father, and whenever His children are facing war, He comes as the Lord of Hosts. Any time you call upon Him if you are facing any battle, it does not matter which song you sing, He will come as a man of war. In 2 Chronicles 20:21-24 when three kings ganged up against Jehoshaphat, he assembled a choir and they sang praises to God. They did not even sing a song of war. They sang that God's mercy endures forever and God replied by destroying the enemies of Jehoshaphat. What do you think He will do when you sing that every knee should bow in the name of Jesus? You can be sure that nothing will be left of your enemy.

You may say you do not know how to sing. All you need to do is to make a joyful noise unto the Lord. All you need do is to shout Alleluia. This is enough to cause all the enemies of God to submit. Psalm 66:1-3 says:

> *"Make a joyful noise unto God, all ye lands: Sing forth the honour of his name: make his praise glorious. Say unto God, How terrible art thou in thy works! through the greatness of thy power shall thine enemies submit themselves unto thee."*

If you can sing, sing. If you cannot sing, make a joyful noise unto the Lord. Your shout will make the enemy tremble because the side that shouts is the winning side.

There are two main ways of getting rid of a demon called poverty. The first way is by giving from the little you have and allow the law of harvest to take control. The second is by praising God. Psalm 67:5-7 confirms this:

> *"Let the people praise thee, O God; let all the people praise thee. Then shall the earth yield her increase; and God, even our own God, shall bless us. God shall bless us; and all the ends of the earth shall fear him."*

If we praise Him, our harvests will be plentiful – indeed, our God shall bless us so much that our neighbours will begin to fear our God.

David is a classic example of someone who was delivered from poverty. He was a shepherd boy who became a king. He started life with no servants but became the controller of a whole nation. No wonder he said in Psalm 32:7:

"Thou art my hiding place; thou shalt preserve me from trouble; thou shalt compass me about with songs of deliverance. Selah."

He knew God had delivered him from enemies that wanted to kill him. He also knew that God had delivered him from brothers who hated him. He knew God had delivered him from a father who never thought he would become anything. He knew God had delivered him from poverty. Everywhere he turned, he saw deliverance. In Psalm 103:1-5, he said:

"Bless the LORD, O my soul: and all that is within me, bless his holy name. Bless the LORD, O my soul, and forget not all his benefits: Who forgiveth all thine iniquities; who healeth all thy diseases; Who redeemeth thy life from destruction; who crowneth thee with lovingkindness and tender mercies; Who satisfieth they mouth with good things; so that they youth is renewed like the eagle's."

Also in Psalm 57:4-7, David said:

"My soul is among lions: and I lie even among them that are set on fire, even the sons of men, whose teeth are spears and arrows, and their tongue a sharp sword. Be thou exalted, O God, above the heavens; let they glory be above all earth. They have prepared a net for my steps; my soul is bowed down: they have digged a pit before me, into the midst whereof they are fallen themselves. Selah. My heart is fixed, O God, my heart is fixed: I will sing and give praise."

The enemies surrounded him. They dug a hole to bury him. He started praising God and it was those who wanted to bury him that were buried. He then said his heart was fixed within him and he would praise the Lord. When David surveyed all that God had done for him, he said in Psalm 34:1-4:

"I will bless the LORD at all times: his praise shall continually be in my mouth. My soul shall make her boast in the LORD: the humble shall hear thereof, and be glad. O magnify the LORD with me, and let us exalt his name together. I sought the LORD, and he heard me, and delivered me from all my fears."

He said he sought the Lord and He heard him and delivered him from all his fears. He said we should magnify the Lord with him and praise His Name together.

Chapter 7

A TESTIMONY ABOUT DAVID

1 Samuel 16:17-18:

> *"And Saul said unto his servants, Provide me now a man that can play well, and bring him to me. Then answered one of the servants, and said, Behold, I have seen a son of Jesse the Bethlehemite, that is cunning in playing, and a mighty valiant man, and a man of war, and prudent in matters, and a comely person, and the LORD is with him."*

Here we have a testimony about David. We will look at this testimony and find out whether such can be written about us. The testimony starts by saying David was a skilful musician and that he was a might man of valour. We are also told that he was a warrior and a prudent man. He was a handsome man and the Lord was with him.

When we say someone is a skilful musician, it means that he or she can either sing very well or is good at playing musical instruments. It is good to know how to play one musical instrument, at least as a sacrifice to God. You can easily learn how to play the tambourine as it is a cheap instrument and readily available. You can use it often in the service. If you do not have the money even to buy a tambourine, there is an instrument that you can play that will not cost you any money. Psalm 47:1 tells us what it is:

"O clap your hands, all ye people; shout unto God with the voice of triumph."

This is one instrument that you can play; everyone can clap. You can clap in such a way as to produce music. There are ways of clapping that will bring glory to God. As a matter of fact, when you are clapping, you are playing a ten-stringed instrument. Psalm 33:1-3 says:

"Rejoice in the LORD, O ye righteous: for praise is comely for the upright. Praise the LORD with harp: sing unto him with the psaltery and an instrument of ten strings. Sing unto him a new song; play skilfully with a loud noise."

We should not regard clapping as merely making a noise. We can clap in a musical way. David was skilful with the harp. We also can be skilful with our hands. We can use them to praise God.

David was also a valiant man. Can you be like him? Of course you can! The Bible tells us the secret of those who are strong in Daniel 11:32:

"And such as do wickedly against the covenant shall he corrupt by flatteries: but the people that do know their God shall be strong, and do exploits."

The people that know God shall be strong and shall do exploits. It is very easy to be strong. All that is required is to know God. All power belongs to God. The moment you know the One who is all powerful you will suddenly discover a new strength.

If the Almighty God is dwelling in you, it follows that, you will be very strong. The Bible tells us in Ephesians 6:10 that we are to be strong in the Lord and in the power of His might. Ephesians 3:14-16 tells us that we are going to be strengthened in the inner man by the Spirit of God. Strength is an inward thing; it always comes from within. The Bible tells us that the joy of the Lord is our strength (Nehemiah 8:10). When your joy is based on the Lord, each time you hear the name of Jesus, joy rises from within you will be strong. The Bible explains how in Isaiah 40:28-31:

"Hast thou not known? hast thou not heard, that the everlasting God, the LORD, the Creator of the ends of the earth, fainteth not, neither is weary? there is no searching of his understanding. He giveth power to the faint; and to them that have no might he increaseth strength. Even the youths shall faint and be weary, and the young men shall utterly fall: But they that wait upon the LORD shall renew their strength; they shall mount up with wings as eagles; they shall run, and not be weary; and they shall walk, and not faint."

What then was the secret of David's strength? It was his constant waiting upon the Lord. Waiting upon the Lord means going before Him, praising and worshipping Him. When you wait on Him like this, no matter what problem you may have, suddenly joy will flood into your being. David was constantly praising God. You can do the same thing. You can praise Him while in the kitchen washing the plates. You can sing choruses to God in the car while you are on your way to work. Suddenly, you will become a mighty man of valour. You will not experience tiredness because the joy of the Lord will constantly renew your strength.

David was also a warrior. We are not just ordinary warriors but chosen warriors. 2 Timothy 2:3-4 says:

"Thou therefore endure hardness, as a good soldier of Jesus Christ. No man that warreth entangleth himself with the affairs of this life; that he may please him who hath chosen him to be a soldier."

We are chosen soldiers of Jesus Christ. In Ephesians 6:12. the Bible calls us spiritual wrestlers. We are wrestling against spiritual forces. If we are soldiers, what then are our weapons? David had no sword. The only weapon that he had was a sling. This, however, was not really his weapon. His weapon was the Name of the Lord. In 1 Samuel 17:45, David said to Goliath:

"Thou comest to me with a sword, and with a spear, and with a shield: but I come to thee in the name of the LORD of hosts, the God of the armies of Israel, whom thou hast defied."

He said he came against Goliath in the Name of the Lord. The Name of the Lord is Jesus Christ. This weapon is also available to us. Jesus Christ said in John 14:14:

"If ye shall ask any thing in my name, I will do it."

You can ask anything in His name. You can ask that all your enemies be vanquished. The Bible summarises the power of the name of Jesus in Philippians 2:9-11, saying that at the name of Jesus, every knee should bow. This is the only weapon that we have. This is why every Christian must be a prayer warrior. The whole armour of God that we are told to wear in Ephesians 6:13-17 can be summarised into one word, JESUS. Our girdle is truth. Jesus Christ is the Truth according to John 14:6. Our breastplate is righteousness and according to Malachi 4:2, Jesus Christ is the Sun of Righteousness. Our boots should be boots of peace and according to Isaiah 9:6, Jesus Christ is the Prince of Peace. Our shield is the shield of faith and according to Hebrews 12:2, Jesus is the Author and Finisher of our faith. Our helmet is the helmet of salvation and according to Matthew 1:21, Jesus is the Saviour. He is our Salvation. The word of God is our sword, and Jesus is the Word of God incarnate, according to John 1:1 and 14:

"In the beginning was the Word, and the Word was with God, and the Word was God."

"And the Word was made flesh, and dwelt among us, (and we beheld his glory, the glory as of the only begotten of the Father,) full of grace and truth."

OUR WHOLE ARMOUR IS *JESUS CHRIST*

David was also a prudent man. He knew how to speak with wisdom. The Bible tells us that Jesus Christ is the wisdom of God. All you have to do is to copy Jesus if you wish to speak with wisdom. There are several examples in the Bible where Jesus was tried but He always replied with wisdom. In John 8:3-11, His enemies tried to ensnare Him with his sayings that He had not come to abolish the law but to fulfil it. They brought to Him a woman caught in the act of fornication and pointed out that according to the law, she had to be stoned to death (John 8:3-8). They asked Him what to do about the matter since He had not come to destroy but to save. This was a trap. If He said the woman should be killed they would question His claim to be the Saviour. If He said they should allow her to go, they would accuse Him of breaking the law. Jesus gave a simple reply, yet full of wisdom. He said that anyone who had never sinned should cast the first stone.

In another passage, some Pharisees came to ask Jesus whether it was lawful for them to pay tax to Caesar. They knew that Caesar ruled their country and that any true Jew would not be happy with this situation. They set him a trap. If Jesus had said it was lawful to pay tax to Caesar, they would have told the other Jews that Jesus was a stooge for the Romans. If He had said it was unlawful to pay tax to Caesar, they would have called Him an insurrectionist. Whatever answer He would have given would have been a trap for Him. Matthew 22:17-22 tells us the full story:

> *"Tell us therefore, What thinkest thou? Is it lawful to give tribute unto Caesar, or not? But Jesus perceived their wickedness, and said, Why tempt ye me, ye hypocrites? Shew me the tribute money. And they brought unto him a penny. And he saith unto them, Whose is this image and superscription? They say unto him, Caesar's. Then saith he unto them, Render therefore unto Caesar the things which are Caesar's; and unto God the things that are God's. When they had heard these words, they marvelled, and left him, and went their way."*

The people who set a trap for Him left marvelling, for His wisdom had confounded them.

In Matthew 21:23-27 Jesus was asked who gave Him the authority to do all the things He was doing. If He had said He was using the authority of God, they would have called Him an imposter since only the High Priest had this authority. If He had said He was using His own authority, they would have accused Him of presumption. He was aware of their trap so He asked them where the authority of John the Baptist came from. They found themselves caught in their own trap and left Him, outwitted again.

Occasionally, you will find yourself face to face with someone who is wiser than you or almost as wise as you are. You are to deal with them just as Jesus dealt with the devil, in Matthew 4:1-11. His reply to all the temptations of the devil was "It is written". Whenever you find yourself in a tight corner, God will give you a Bible passage that you will quote. Two of my friends once came to me to ask which of the two should lead. Maybe they wanted to put me in a tight corner but God gave me wisdom. Romans 12:10 says we should prefer one another in honour. This means that you should put your friend first when it comes to honour. I threw the ball back into their court.

Why not tell the devil something of what you know about the word of God? It is written that you are not going to die but live to declare the glory of God. It is written that it shall be well with the righteous, so you will be prosperous in all aspects of your life.

It is written that the Lord will never fail those who trust in Him, so if you trust in Him He will never fail you. It is written that everywhere you go He will be with you because He will never leave you or forsake you. It is written that at the name of Jesus, every knee must bow, so failure, illness and their likes have no place in your life.

If you are not yet a Christian, it is written that unless you are born again you will not see the Kingdom of God. Taste and see that the Lord is good.

Chapter 8

---◆◆◆---

DIVINE PRESENCE

1 Samuel 16:17-18:

> *"And Saul said unto his servants, Provide me now a man that can play well, and bring him to me. Then answered one of the servants, and said, Behold, I have seen a son of Jesse the Bethlehemite, that is cunning in playing, and a mighty valiant man, and a man of war, and prudent in matters, and a comely person, and the LORD is with him."*

Divine Presence spells Blessings untold

David was a handsome person but God did not choose him because he was handsome. As a matter of fact, physical beauty is irrelevant when it comes to God's dealings. The kind of beauty that God has interest in is the inner beauty. Proverbs 31:30 has this to say:

> *"Favour is deceitful, and beauty is vain: but a woman that feareth the LORD, she shall be praised."*

God is not interested in outward beauty that does not come from inner beauty. He is only concerned with in the beauty that radiates from within to the outside. Those whose inner man has been beautified do not worry much about outward beauty. Much of the cosmetic surgery that we have done to our bodies are insults to God. What we are telling God is that He did not do a perfect job and we want to help Him.

When your spirit is in absolute surrender to the Almighty God, you will not care about what anybody may say about your outward appearance. Also, many of the things that we do wear to adorn ourselves are symbols of pride; Our attempts to make ourselves beautiful can get us into trouble with God. The inner beauty is called the beauty of holiness in Psalm 110:3:

> *"Thy people shall be willing in the day of thy power, in the beauties of holiness from the womb of the morning: thou hast the dew of thy youth."*

Psalm 149:4 says:

> *"For the LORD taketh pleasure in his people: he will beautify the meek with salvation."*

God will beautify you with salvation. God will beautify anyone who is truly born again and ready to receive this meekness from God.

We are also told that God was with David. When God is with someone, several things follow. The first thing that follows is that God is backing you up. When God is backing you up, you will go from success to success. A man can do the impossible if he has the backing of God.

When God told Moses in Exodus 3 that he should lead the children of Israel out of Egypt, Moses laughed. However, God told Moses that He would be with him. This made all the difference. When God promoted Joshua from a messenger to President and He told him to take over from Moses and lead the people to the Promised Land, Joshua thought God was joking. God told him in Joshua 1:5 that just as He was with Moses He will be with Him. When God called Gideon in Judges 6 to rise up and deliver Israel, Gideon was very hesitant until God said He would be with him. The Bible in Acts 10:38 attributes every miracle that Jesus performed to the fact that God was with Him.

When God is backing you up, opposition will crumble. You will do mighty things and people will want to know your secret. The secret is that God is with you. When you sing and souls are saved, it can only mean that God is with you. If you start off selling water and ends up a millionaire, it is because God is with you.

Divine protection is also guaranteed if God is with you. God said in Isaiah 43:2:

"When thou passest through the waters, I will be with thee; and through the rivers, they shall not overflow thee: when thou walkest through the fire, thou shalt not be burned; neither shall the flame kindle upon thee."

In Daniel 3:23-25, the Bible says that when Shadrach, Meshach and Abednego were cast into the fiery furnace, the only thing that was burnt was the rope that bound them. This was because God was with them. If God is with you, any fire that the enemy may prepare for you will only burn the things that are biding you in your life. When God is with you, any enemy that sees you will see that God is with you. When they come against you from one direction, they will run away from you in seven.

If God is with you, you will be able to say like David said in Psalm 23:4:

"Yea, though I walk through the valley of the shadow of death, I will fear no evil: for thou art with me, thy rod and thy staff they comfort me."

If God is with you, when the time comes to go, you will sing all the way home.

We discover in Genesis 39:2-5 something very interesting:

"And the Lord was with Joseph, and he was a prosperous man; and he was in the house of his master the Egyptian. And his master saw that the Lord was with him, and that the Lord made all that he did to prosper in his hand. And Joseph found grace in his sight, and he served him: and he made him overseer over his house, and all that he had he put into his hand. And it came to pass from the time that he had made him overseer in his house, and over all that he had, that the Lord blessed the Egyptian's house for Joseph's sake; and the blessing of the Lord was upon all that he had in the house, and in the field."

The Lord was with Joseph and he prospered. When God is with you, you too will prosper. When God is helping, there is no task that will be difficult. When

God is with you, nobody will be able to stop you from rising up. Psalm 5:12 says:

"For thou, LORD, wilt bless the righteous; with favour wilt thou compass him as with a shield."

Proverbs 3:33 says:

"The curse of the LORD is in the house of the wicked: but he blesseth the habitation of the just."

If God is with you, it follows that you must be just. It means you are doing His pleasure. The Bible says God blessed the house of Potiphar for Joseph's sake. When God is with you, anybody you meet will be blessed. Proverbs 28:20 says:

"A faithful man shall abound with blessings: but he that maketh haste to be rich shall not be innocent."

Your blessings will overflow. They will be so abundant that people will be able to steal part of it without you even knowing.

Divine favour also follows if God is with you. Grace was upon Joseph. Everything he did pleased his master. Divine favour is a wonderful thing. You should pray to God every morning for favour. In Genesis 6:8, the Bible says Noah found grace with God and as a result, when God was about to destroy the whole world, He spared Noah and his family. May you find grace with God.

Mary was just an ordinary girl, a virgin, like many girls of her age, but in Luke 1:30 the Bible tells us that Mary found grace with God. God chose her out of many thousands and she became forever special. When God was talking to Paul in 2 Corinthians 12:9, He told him His grace was sufficient for him. If you have the grace of God, everything else is easy.

When God is with you, you will begin to rise up supernaturally. As a slave, Joseph became overseer. He took over the house. It was he who decided what the master would eat. He received supernatural promotion. Psalm 75:6-7 tells us that promotion comes from God:

"For promotion cometh neither from the east, nor from the west, nor from

the south. But God is the judge: he putteth down one, and setteth up another."

In Genesis 39:20-23, the Bible makes it clear that when they threw Joseph into prison, the jailer made him the overseer of all the other prisoners because God was with him. If God is with you, wherever you are, you will succeed.

DIVINE ABSENCE SPELLS DOOM

If God withdraws from you, trouble will follow. The Bible tells us in Romans 8:31 that if God is for us, who can be against us? This also means if God is against us, who can be for us? If God is supporting you, let the whole world come against you – they will fall down flat before you. However, if God is against you, even if your Pastor prays and fasts for you, it will still make no difference. I pray that God will never be against you.

In Joshua 7:10-12, we learn an important lesson. When God was with Joshua and the children of Israel, the wall of Jericho fell down. All they did was to shout and the mighty wall collapsed enabling them to destroy the city. After this victory, they faced a small town called Ai and the people of Ai chased them and killed 36 of them. Joshua fell on his face and asked God the reason for their fall God old him that it was because He was no longer with them, for they had brought sin into their camp. This is why I always talk about holiness. If you are living holy lives, God will be with you. If God is with you, you will have victory upon victory, success upon success and everything will be easy for you. As a Christian, if you are doing the things that will keep God away from you, you will face all manner of trouble. Christianity without the presence of Christ will always lead you to crisis.

In 1 Samuel 4:3-11, the children of God were fighting against the Philistines and the Philistines defeated them. They decided to send for the ark of the Lord. The two people carrying the ark were wicked men. The ark arrived in the camp but God was not there, even though its arrival made the people happy. When the Philistines heard, they trembled, but stirred themselves, and the ark was captured. Some of us put the Bible on our chest or under our pillows when we want to sleep. If God is not in your heart, the Bible is just an ordinary book. If God is with you, your protection is sure.

We all know the story of Samson in Judges 16:20-21. His name made his enemies tremble when God was with him. When God was with him, he tore a lion as if it was a little goat. When God was with him, he uprooted the gate of a city. When God was with him, he used the jawbone of an ass to kill a thousand people. After God left him, the Philistines took him and plucked out his eyes. He tried to fight but his strength had gone. That is why you must pray to God that you will never do anything that might make Him to leave you, He should not let you do it.

However, if you are not a Christian, how can you say that God is with you when you are His enemy? Become His friend. Give your life to Jesus Christ today. He will save your soul and begin to live in you, so that and everywhere you go, you will be able to say, "The Lord is with me."

Chapter 9

BEING A DIVINE CHAMPION

1 Samuel 17:1-11:

"Now the Philistines gathered together their armies to battle, and were gathered together in Shochoh, which belongeth to Judah, and pitched between Shochoh and Azekah, in Ephesdammim. And Saul and the men of Israel were gathered together, and pitched by the valley of Elah, and set the battle in array against the Philistines. And the Philistines stood on a mountain on the one side, and Israel stood on a mountain on the other side: and there was a valley between them. And then went out a champion out of the camp of the Philistines, named Goliath, of Gath, whose height was six cubits and a span. And he had an helmet of brass upon his head, and he was armed with a coat of mail; and the weight of the coat was five thousand shekels of brass. And he had greaves of brass upon his legs and a target of brass between his shoulders. And the staff of his spear was like a weaver's beam; and his spear's head weighed six hundred shekels of iron: and one bearing a shield went before him. And he stood and cried unto the armies of Israel, and said unto them, Why are ye come out to set your battle in array? Am not I a Philistine, and ye servants to Saul? Choose you a man

for you, and let him come down to me. If he be able to fight with me, and to kill me, then will we be your servants: but if I prevail against him, and kill him, then shall ye be our servants, and serve us. And the Philistine said, I defy the armies of Israel this day; give me a man that we may fight together. When Saul and all Israel heard those words of the Philistine, they were dismayed, and greatly afraid."

WHAT IT TAKES TO BE A DIVINE CHAMPION

What is a champion? A champion is a representative of a group of people, as we find in the passage above. Goliath came as a champion for the Philistines and he wanted the children of Israel to choose one man to be their champion. Once a champion is defeated, it follows that the people he is representing have been defeated. Thank God that our champion is Jesus Christ. He has never been defeated and that is why we are winners all the time. God is looking for champions to represent Him against demons and forces of darkness. He is looking for men and women who will stand up against the devil and challenge him and his representatives.

To become a divine champion, you must have certain characteristics.

(i) Anyone that God will use as a champion must believe deeply within themselves that one with God is a majority (Romans 8:31). That once you have God with you, you have won. Divine mathematics is quite different from human. Numbers always impresses us but God is not impressed by how many of us are going to battle. We have an example in the case of Gideon. God does not do addition. He does multiplication. When we are talking about a man and his wife, we call them two but God calls them one $(1 + 1 = 1$ and not $1 + 1 = 2)$. When we are talking about one with God, it is not one plus God but one multiplied by God. The result will be God and God has never lost a battle. In 1 Kings 18, we saw Elijah, a champion of God, standing on Mount Carmel, face to face with 850 prophets of Baal. As far as we are concerned, we will say, 850 versus one. The equation was actually 850 versus one multiplied by God. When God is the one controlling that one person, the result is always victory. God is not concerned with how many people but with what kind of people. God is not interested in what you can do but in what He can do through you. What will determine the success of any group of people is not the size of the group but the size of their God. The God that we serve is a great God; the problem with many of us is that we are not properly joined to God all the time.

(ii) Anyone wishing to become a champion must never be concerned with the problem. His interest must be in the potential available for him to solve problems. Philippians 4:13 says:

"I can do all things through Christ which strengtheneth me."

Moses sent twelve people to survey the Promised Land (Numbers 13). Ten of them returned with a report that although the land was full of milk and honey, there were giants there. The other two said they could take the land if God was on their side. Many a time, we find ourselves faced with great opportunities that are brilliantly disguised as problems. In fact, God uses problems to toughen us so that we can progress. When many of us think of what God can do, we think of those things we know are possible, by our standards, whereas, the Bible says in Luke 1:37:

"For with God nothing shall be impossible."

Likewise, many of our prayers are based on what we think God can do. In reality, there is nothing God cannot do.

(iii) The focus of a divine champion is not on his ability but on the fact that he is available. Ability belongs to God and not to us. Psalm 62:11 says:

"God hath spoken one; twice have I heard this; that power belongeth unto God."

Job said in Job 42:2:

"I know that thou canst do everything, and that no thought can be withholden from thee."

All that God is asking is whether or not you are available so that through you, He can display His ability. Many of us think that God wants us to be a soul winner. However, you are not the Saviour, merely the messenger who tells people what God is doing.

1 Corinthians 4:2 says:

"Moreover it is required in stewards, that a man be found faithful."

All that God wants from you is faithfulness. He is not asking you to be spectacular, gifted or brilliant. God is not asking you to be an orator, just a faithful Christian.

(iv) God will use a man who is willing to be obedient to the letter. This is one of the reasons why God uses people who are unknown. When He commands them, they will obey. They do not argue with God. In 1 Kings 17:1-3, God said to Elijah – one of His champions – to go and hide, so this is what he did – without questioning. He obeyed God to the letter.

(v) God will use a man or woman who will be loyal to the very end, God is looking for loyalty. It is disloyalty that makes some people run from one church to the other. God cannot use people like Gehazi who was ready to take the money that his master rejected. The Bible says in Revelation 2:10:

"Fear none of those things which thou shalt suffer: behold, the devil shall cast some of you into prison, that ye may be tried; and ye shall have tribulation ten days: be thou faithful unto death, and I will give thee a crown of life."

God is still looking for divine champions. He is still looking for people to send. Will you go for Him?

Chapter 10

---◆◆◆---

THE SINFUL HAVE CAUSE TO FEAR

1 Samuel 17:10-11:

> *"And the Philistine said, I defy the armies of Israel this day; give me a man, that we may fight together. When Saul and all Israel heard those words of the Philistine, they were dismayed, and greatly afraid."*

Saul was an anointed man of God. If you are anointed, you are supposed to be impregnable. In fact, the word of God says, "Touch not mine anointed" (Psalm 105:15). If God says that you are His anointed and that He is with you, then you should have nothing to fear. As the Scriptures tell us in Romans 8:31, if God is for you, who can be against you? Psalm 24:7-10 tells us that our God is also called the Lord of hosts. He is the Captain of the hosts of Heaven. If the Commander-in-Chief is your friend, why should you be afraid of a Captain? All your friend has to do is to tell the Captain to get out of the way and he dare not disobey. In fact, the word of God tells us in Deuteronomy 28:2 and 7:

> *"And all these blessings shall come on thee, and overtake thee, if thou shalt hearken unto the voice of the LORD they God."*

> *"The LORD shall cause thine enemies that rise up against thee to be smitten*

54

before thy face: they shall come out against thee one way, and flee before thee seven ways."

If you are a child of God, it is impossible for you to become demon-possessed. How can the demon get inside you? He may come against you one way, but will end up fleeing seven ways. When the enemy is coming against you and suddenly sees the Lord of hosts behind you, unless he is crazy, he will run. However, if you dabble into sin, then it is you who should run.

If you dabble with sin, it separates you from God. You will be separated from your Defender. This is why King Saul trembled. When he was obeying God, he was able to chase the Philistines out of Israel. He became the captain of the army of God. Even his son, Jonathan, aided only by his armour bearer, destroyed a whole garrison of the Philistines.

When God is with you, your enemy will become your footstool. When there is no sin in your life, you will be friends with God. Holiness is the secret of success, security, peace, and blessing. If God is with you, everything you touch will succeed because He will teach you what to do, and no enemy will be able to withstand you. Let us take the example of Adam in Genesis 2:19-20:

"And out on the ground the LORD God formed every beast of the field, and even fowl of the air; and brought them unto Adam to see what he would call them: and whatsoever Adam called every living creature, that was the name thereof. And Adam gave names to all cattle, and to the fowl of the air, and to every beast of the field; but for Adam there was not found an help meet for him."

Before the fall, God told Adam, to name the creatures He had created. God did not overrule Adam's choice of names. The implication here is that when you are in close fellowship with God, God will back anything you say. When Jesus says yes, nobody can say no. When you are in fellowship with God, you will always succeed. In Genesis 3:9-10 the picture is very different:

"And the LORD God called unto Adam, and said unto him, Where art thou? And he said, I heard thy voice in the garden, and I was afraid, because I was naked; and I hid myself."

Here when Adam heard the voice of God he was afraid. This was a very different reaction to what we read in the previous chapter. When you are living a life of holiness, you always rejoice when you come into the house of God, but when you are living in sin, you do not want to hear the voice of the Lord. Sin destroys that intimacy. In Genesis 3:8 the Bible says:

"And they heard the voice of the Lord God walking in the garden in the cool of the day: and Adam and his wife hid themselves from the presence of the Lord God amongst the trees of the garden."

God wanted to have fellowship with Adam and Eve but they hid from Him. I want God to be with me. I want God to be with me everywhere I go. If you allow God to be with you, doors will begin to open automatically. However, if you sin, even if you ask Him to be with you, He will not come because He is a Holy God and the Bible tells us in Isaiah 59:1-2:

"Behold, the LORD's hand is not shortened, that it cannot save; neither his ear heavy, that it cannot hear: But your iniquities have separated between you and your God, and your sins have hid his face from you that he will not hear."

Sin brings separation. It also brings shame. Look at Genesis 2:25:

"And they were naked, the man and his wife, and were not ashamed."

Before they sinned, they were naked yet they felt no shame because the glory of God covered them. However, in Genesis 3:7 things had changed:

"And the eyes of them both were opened, and they knew that they were naked; and they sewed fig leaves together, and made themselves aprons."

You can see here how terrible sin is. They were once covered by the glory of God and did not know what we call shame, but when they sinned, they began to look for something to cover their shame. They used leaves that would be green in the morning and dry in the evening. Sin will take away the glory of God and replace it with leaves. Sin also causes defeat. This was why King Saul was afraid. He knew that if he went to battle against Goliath, he would be defeated. We see another example of this in Joshua 7:10-12, after the great victory of Jericho, Joshua led his people to attack a small village called Ai and they were defeated. They were defeated because there was sin in their camp. God told Joshua to remove sin from the camp and He would continue to be with them.

HOLINESS PRODUCES DIVINE BOLDNESS

You leave yourself open to defeat when you sin. Even a minor transgression will cause you to fall. On the other hand, if you are living a life of holiness, you will be bold. Proverbs 28:1 puts this very succinctly:

> *"The wicked flee when no man pursueth: but the righteous are bold as a lion."*

When you sin, even when nobody is even chasing you at all, you run away. You will see your shadow and think that it is an armed robber. You will hear the wind blowing and believe that demons have come. In reality you have nothing to fear except sin. You can fear God by running away from sin. If you do not sin, I can assure you that God will treat you as a beloved child. If you do not do anything wrong, God will talk to you as a friend. If you only keep away from sin, there is nothing else to fear. The righteous man is as bold as a lion because he knows what is already written in Isaiah 3:10:

> *"Say ye to the righteous that it shall be well with him: for they shall eat the fruit of their doings."*

Once you start living a holy life, it is going to be well with you. When you are living a life of holiness, you will be able to abide under the shadow of the Almighty God. There will be nothing to separate you from God. He will cover you with His wings. Psalm 91:4-11 says:

> *"He shall cover thee with his feathers, and under his wings shalt thou trust: his truth shall be they shield and buckler. Thou shalt not be afraid for the terror by night; nor for the arrow that flieth by day: Nor for the pestilence that walketh in darkness; nor for the destruction that wasteth at noonday. A thousand shall fall at thy side an ten thousand at thy right hand; but it shall not come nigh thee. Only with thine eyes shalt thou behold and see the reward of the wicked. Because thou hast made the LORD, which is my refuge, even the most High, thy habitation; There shall no evil befall thee,*

neither shall any plague come nigh thy dwelling. For he shall give his angels charge over thee, to keep thee in all thy ways."

When you are living a life of holiness, you have angels as your bodyguards and they will go with you everywhere you go. They will see danger miles off and ensure you are protected. The Bible says in Proverbs 18:10:

"The name of the LORD is a strong tower: the righteous runneth into it, and is safe."

There is security in the name of the Lord. Psalm 125:1-3 says:

"They that trust in the LORD shall be as mount Zion, which cannot be removed, but abideth forever. As the mountains are round about Jerusalem, so the LORD is round about his people from henceforth even for ever. For the rod of the wicked shall not rest upon the lot of the righteous; lest the righteous put forth their hands unto iniquity."

This passage is simply saying that if you are living a life of holiness you will stand firm, and need not be afraid because nothing can move you. Nothing happens without God's permission. You cannot even suck an orange without God's permission. You cannot do anything unless God permits it. The devil cannot do anything either unless God permits it. No demon can come near you except God permits it. If you are living holy lives, God is not going to allow the wicked to come near you to discourage you. In Hebrews 1:9, the Bible says:

"Thou hast loved righteousness, and hated iniquity; therefore God, even they God, hath anointed thee with the oil of gladness above thy fellows."

Those who are living holy lives do not even need to pray for anointing. The anointing will come, and when you are anointed, according to Isaiah 10:27, that anointing breaks the yoke. This means that even if we assume that demons can bind you, the anointing will break the yoke. In reality, if you are living a holy life no demon can bind you. In Judges 15:11-14, we note that it was not the enemy that bound Samson but his kinsmen. For instance, if a member of your family or an evil person puts you under spiritual bondage, when the anointing of God comes, all bondage will be broken.

Chapter 11

AGE AND DIVINE CALL

1 Samuel 17:12-21:

"Now David was the son of that Ephrathite of Bethlehem Judah, whose name was Jesse; and he had eight sons: And the man went among men for an old man in the days of Saul. And the three eldest sons of Jesse went and followed Saul to the battle: and the names of his three sons that went to the battle were Eliab the first born, and next unto him Abinadab, and the third Shammah. And David was the youngest: and the three eldest followed Saul. But David went and returned from Saul to feed his father's sheep at Bethlehem. And the Philistine drew near morning and evening, and presented himself forty days. And Jesse said unto David his son, Take now for they brethren an ephah of this parched corn, and these ten loaves, and run to the camp to thy brethren; And carry these ten loaves, and run to the camp to thy brethren; And carry these ten cheeses unto the captain of their thousand, and look how thy brethren fare, and take their pledge. Now Saul, and they, and all the men of Israel; were on the valley of Elah, fighting with the Philistines. And David rose up early in the morning, and left the sheep with a keeper, and took, and went, as Jesse had commanded him; and he

came to the trench, as the host was going forth to the fight, and shouted for the battle. For Israel and the Philistines had put the battle in array, army against army."

AGE HAS NOTHING TO DO WITH DIVINE CALL

Jesse had eight sons and David was the youngest. He was the last born and yet it pleased the Almighty God to choose him for service. Moses had an elder brother called Aaron (Exodus 4:14) and he had an elder sister called Miriam (Exodus 2:2-4). This means that Moses was at least number three in the family. He was not the firstborn. When his mother sent him floating down the River Nile, his sister was already old enough to look after him. This means that whether you are the firstborn or the youngest does not really matter. Joseph was the second youngest in his family, according to Genesis 35:24. On the other hand, John the Baptist was the firstborn, according to Luke 1:5-7 and 13. There is no record that his parents had another child. This means that God can call any of us for service. It means that we are all qualified by God's grace for a divine call.

God can call you at any time, as we see in 1 Samuel 3:1-4. Samuel was a child when God called him. When we are talking of age, neither physical age nor spiritual age are necessarily restrictions. In other words, you can be born again today and God can call you today. Samuel was a child and God called him. I felt the call of God for the first time, when I was less than two years old spiritually. According to Deuteronomy 34:7, Moses was 120 years old when he died and according to Numbers 14:33, the Bible said the children of Israel wandered in the wilderness for 40 years. This means that Moses was 80 years old when God called him. In other words, at the time you are thinking of retiring God may decide He is about to begin with you. You are not too old to be used by God. You are not too young to be used by God.

In Genesis 12:4, We observe that Abraham was called at the age of 75. He began his work with God when he was quite elderly and he was still walking with God when he was more than a hundred years old. However, in Genesis 5:25-27, the Bible tells us that Methuselah was 969 years old he died. He was almost 1000 years old but all we read about him was that he lived and had sons and daughters, and died. He had very little to show for his 969 years. If God was to write about you today, what would He write? Would it be just that you lived, you ate, you drank and you died? Pray that God will not let you drift through life. Wake up, because God is recording everything we are doing for Him.

WE ALL START AS INFANTS, BUT WHILE SOME BECOME KINGS, OTHERS OF US END UP AS SERVANTS

Everyone that you ever read about, started life as a baby. Later in life some become kings, or presidents or somebody great while others end up as servants, messengers or a cleaners. Please do not misunderstand me, if you are a cleaner in the house of God, as far as God is concerned, you are greater than a president who does not know Jesus. What matters is that what you do you are doing for God.

We likewise all start as infants in the Lord, and while some end up raising the dead, opening blind eyes, winning souls for Christ, others never end up doing anything or becoming anything for God. Why is this? There are two major factors. The first one is divine plan and the second one is personal responsibility. Romans 9:16 says:

> *"So then it is not of him that willeth, nor of him that runneth but of God that sheweth mercy."*

You should be thrilled that God set His love upon you? If He did not love you, you would still be dead in your sins. God the Father called you and you responded. In Jeremiah 1:4-5, we read:

> *"Then the word of the LORD came unto me, saying, Before I formed thee in the belly, I knew thee; and before thou comest forth out of the womb I sanctified thee, and I ordained thee a prophet unto the nations."*

Before you father met your mother, God had mapped out His plans for your life. Should you not be pleased that it is a good plan? If He planned anything contrary to what is happening to you now, there is nothing you can do, God is in the heavens and He does as He pleases. It has however pleased Him to call you unto salvation. It has pleased Him to make you a child of God. It has pleased Him to ensure you will be one of those who will reach Heaven.

Paul said in Galatians 1:13-16 that in his earlier years when he was known as Saul of Tarsus, he persecuted the Church and fought against Jesus Christ. God, however, was watching because He had a plan for his life. He knew that from his mother's womb he had been separated to become a vessel of honour in His hands.

When God has a plan concerning you, it does not matter what may have happened in the past, His plan will still come to pass. When the time came, He told Saul that enough was enough. Many of us have similar stories to tell. Many of us were on the road to Hell but this was not the plan of God. The plan of God for our lives is that we will end up in Heaven. Divine plans will always require divine intervention. This was why when Saul of Tarsus was going to Damascus in Acts 9:1-7, God met him on the way and told him that the time had come.

One can then ask why we should blame Esau for what he did, when the Bible says that before Esau and Jacob were born, God had decided which one to love and which one to hate. God knows the end from the beginning. He knew that Esau was going to sell his birthright. God also knows those who will do His will. In 1 Samuel 13:13-14, the Bible records thus:

"And Samuel said to Saul, Thou hast done foolishly: thou hast not kept the commandments of the LORD thy God, which he commanded thee: for now would the LORD have established thy kingdom upon Israel forever. But now they kingdom shall not continue: the LORD hath sought him a man after his own heart, and the LORD hath commanded him to be captain over his people, because thou hast not kept that which the LORD commanded thee."

King Saul never thought that he would become a king. In fact, when he was told that he was going to be made a king, he said his family was the least in Israel, but God said this was not a problem. When he attained the position of king, he failed to please God and God changed the plan, because He is the Almighty.

It may appear that you will die a poor person but if God sees that you want to serve Him. He can change the tide, In Proverbs 8:17, God said:

"I love them that love me; and those that seek me early shall find me."

God loves those that love Him. In other words, if you make up your mind today that you will love God with all your body, soul and spirit, and serve Him, He will love you in return. God will not hate you if you love Him. If you decide to love Him, He will love you in return. If you decide to serve Him, He will give you what you need for the task. Acts 10:34-35 says:

"Then Peter opened his mouth, and said, Of a truth I perceive that God is no respecter of persons: But in every nation he that feareth him, and worketh righteousness, is accepted with him."

In every nation, He will accept anyone who will fear Him and walk in righteousness. We were all born as spiritual infants. Some of us end up as spiritual giants while some will end up as spiritual nonentities. God has His plans but you also have your own responsibilities. I know that God has a great plan for your life. I also know that you can spoil that plan. You can tell God that you do not love Him and you do not want to serve and please Him. God will do whatever you want.

There may be some people who will not become a Pastor but will be so full of the power of God that they only have to breathe out, miracles will happen. It is up to you what you want to become for God. I am not going to end up as a nobody. I am going to end up as a giant for the Lord. You will have to make your own choice.

If you have not yet believed on Jesus, the way that you begin your walk with God is by giving your life to Jesus Christ. If you are already a Christian, thank God for His plans for you and ask Him to let you love Him more.

Chapter 12

REACHING YOUR GOAL

1 Samuel 17:16, 22-30:

"And the Philistine drew near morning and evening, and presented himself forty days."

"And David left his carriage in the hand of the keeper of the carriage, and ran into the army, and came and saluted his brethren. And as he talked with them, behold, there came up the champion, the Philistine of Gath, Goliath by name, out of the armies of the Philistines, and spake according to the same words: and David heard them. And all the men of Israel, when they saw the man, fled from him, and were sore afraid. And the men of Israel said, Have ye seen this man that is come up? Surely to defy Israel is he come up: and it shall be, that the man who killeth him, the king will enrich him with great riches, and will give him his daughter, and make his father's house free in Israel. And David spake to the men that stood by him, saying, What shall be done to the man that killeth this Philistine, and taketh away the reproach from Israel? For who is this uncircumcised Philistine, that he should defy the armies of the living God? And the people answered him after this manner, saying, So shall it be done to the man that killeth him.

*And Eliab his eldest brother heard when he spake unto the men; and Eliab's
anger was kindled against David, and he said, Why comest thou down
hither? And with whom hast thou left those few sheep in the wilderness?
I know thy pride, and the naughtiness of thine heart; for thou art come
down that thou mightest see the battle, And David said, What have I now
done? Is there not a cause? And he turned from him toward another and
spake after the same manner: and the people answered him again after
the former manner."*

Goliath had been terrorising the children of Israel, challenging anyone among
them who could fight him to come forward. His opponent would be Israel's
champion while he would be the champion of the Philistines. Everybody fled
from him. Jesse asked David to take some food to his brethren who were in the
army and by the time he got there, Goliath was striding forth, making his
announcement as usual. David asked what would be done for the person who
could kill Goliath. He was told that the King would grant him great riches, and
his daughter in marriage, while his family would never pay tax again.

Eliab heard David talking and he rebuked him. Eliab had not forgotten what
happened some days earlier, when he thought that he would be chosen as
king but he was rejected and David was anointed instead. He had been envious
of him since then. David turned from him and asked again what would be the
reward for the person who kills Goliath.

TO REACH YOUR GOAL YOU MUST JUST PRESS ON.

Goliath had terrorised the children of Israel for forty days. You may be having
problems now, but I want to prophesy to you that it will not last more than forty
days. Psalm 30:5 says:

*"For his anger endureth but a moment; in his favour is life: weeping may
endure for a night, but joy cometh in the morning."*

Isaiah 3:10 says:

*"Say ye to the righteous that it shall be well with him: for they shall eat the
fruit of their doings."*

I am sure that my future will be bright. I am also sure that your future will be bright. If your enemies are already rejoicing, I want you to know that the rejoicing of the enemies will not last. If you are one hundred percent on the side of God, not only will the joy of the enemy be short-lived, but they will be silenced forever.

When Daniel was thrown in the lions' den in Daniel 6, his enemies were rejoicing. I am sure that the night Daniel was in the lions' den, his enemies probably held a party. However, by the following morning, they were food for lions.

Eliab was angry with David because he was jealous. David had been chosen as king while he had been rejected by God. We often meet people who are jealous. Jealousy is a very dangerous thing. In Song of Sons 8:6:

> *"Set me as a seal upon thine heart, as a seal upon thine arm: for love is strong as death; jealousy is cruel as the grave: the coals thereof are coals of fire, which hath a most vehement flame."*

Jealousy is as cruel as the grave. In other words, a jealous person can become a killer. Any time you find that somebody is more successful than you are, the best thing to do is to continue to pray for them and ask the Almighty God not to forget you. If you wish that it will be well with somebody else, surely, it will be well with you too. If you become jealous and you begin to wish that someone should not prosper, or that he will crumble, then you will be destroying yourself because of the law of harvest. The Bible tells us that a man's enemy will be of his household, according to Matthew 10:36. Eliab was the one who began to reproach David. He wanted to rob David of one of the greatest blessings of his life, but he did not succeed. It does not matter where your enemies are coming from; if the Lord is with you, no one will be able to stand against you.

We should also notice the response of David. David ignored Eliab. Anyone who wants to reach their goal must not be deterred by criticism. If you want to work for God, you must not listen to what others are saying. Whether they are praising you or criticising you, close your ears to both. Focus your attention on the Almighty God. This is the only way to reach your goal. Psalm 1:1 says:

"Blessed is the man that walketh not in the counsel of the ungodly, nor standeth in the way of sinners, nor sitteth in the seat of the scornful."

Do not sit down with the scornful. Some people have no goals and they do not want those who have goals to succeed, so they tell them that they cannot make it. Tell them that you can make it. Do not listen to criticisms or else you will not be able to serve the Lord. Do not listen to praises or else you will become proud and God will begin to resist you. You are not working for man so the praises of men are irrelevant. You are not working for man so the criticisms of men are also irrelevant. The Bible tells us in 2 Timothy 2:4 that anyone who is warring must not allow anything to entangle him:

"No man that warreth entangleth himself with the affairs of this life; that he may please him who hath chosen him to be soldier."

Hebrews 12:2 says:

"Looking unto Jesus the author and finisher of our faith; who for the joy that was set before him endured the cross, despising the shame, and is set down at the right hand of the throne of God."

In Philippians 3:13-14, Paul said:

"Brethren, I count not myself to have apprehended: but this one thing I do, forgetting those things which are behind, and reaching forth unto those things which are before, I press toward the mark for the prize of the high calling of God in Christ Jesus."

If you want to reach your goal, press on. To press on implies that you might face resistance. There will be those who want to slow you down but you have to push them out of the way and keep doing what you know God wants you to do. David asked the people what the reward was for the person who would kill Goliath, the uncircumcised Philistine.

In Genesis 17:1-16, the Almighty God entered into a covenant with Abraham and God said that the evidence of the covenant between the two of them was that all male children in the family should be circumcised. Anyone who was not circumcised would have no part in the covenant. When David said "This uncircumcised Philistine," he was saying Goliath was not part of this covenant.

A covenant is not an ordinary agreement or contract. A covenant is a matter of life and death. If you break a covenant, you will die. God can never break His covenant. He said that Abraham will become the father of many nations, and this is being fulfilled, Romans 2:28-29 states clearly that this covenant has been extended to us. Originally, it was meant for the Jews only but today, as many as are born again, share the blessings of the Jews. According to Galatians 3:13-14, the blessings of Abraham have become part of our blessings. According to Numbers 23:19, God is not a man that He should lie. Once He has spoken, it will happen. Once He enters into a covenant with you, that covenant is settled. He cannot break it unless you break it.

This is one of the reasons why every true child of God should know beyond any doubt that they are already blessed. As long as you keep the covenant between you and God, even if the devil may hide the blessing, one day, it will come to the surface.

THERE ARE REWARDS FOR VICTORS

David asked what the rewards were I want you to know that God does not ask you to fight battles for nothing. Each time you fight and win, He will reward you. This is His way. There are always rewards for those who overcome. We will look at a few of the rewards. Revelation 2:7 says:

> *"He that hath an ear, let him hear what the Spirit saith unto the churches: To him that overcometh will I give to eat of the tree of life, which is in the midst of the paradise of God."*

Why did Adam and Eve get into trouble? They ate from the tree of the knowledge of good and evil. There was one more tree, they had not tasted. God drove them out so as not to eat from this tree, the tree of life. Those of us who overcome will eat from the tree of life. Revelation 2:11 says:

> *"He that hath an ear, let him hear what the Spirit saith unto the churches; He that overcometh shall not be hurt of the second death."*

Anyone whose name is not found in the book of life will be thrown into the lake of fire. This is the second death. Anyone who overcomes will never go into the lake of fire. If you have ever touched fire, you will thank God for the rest of your life that you are not going to Hell.

Revelation 2:17 says:

> *"To him that overcometh will give to eat of the hidden manna, and will give him a white stone, and in the stone a new name written, which no man knoweth saving he that receiveth it."*

The children of Israel ate manna in the wilderness. The Bible calls this the food of angels. Those who overcome will eat of this manna when they get to Heaven. Any food that is good enough for angels must be very special.

The passage goes further to say that those who overcome will be given a white stone on which is written a name that will only be known to the recipient. I do not know what Jesus is going to write on that white stone but it is one thing you are not even going to share with your best friend. Maybe what He will write on my stone is, "You are the one I love most". In Revelation 2:26, the Bible says:

> *"And he that overcometh, and keepeth my works unto the end, to him will I give power over the nations."*

We are going to reign with Jesus Christ. Some of us will be council chairmen, not by election, but by divine decree. There will be those who will be governors, commissioners and presidents. He will give us power over the nations. In Revelation 3:5, we read of another reward:

> *"He that overcometh, the same shall be clothed in white raiment; and I will not blot out his name out of the book of life, but I will confess his name before my Father, and before his angels."*

When you get to Heaven, you are going to be clothed in white. Jesus will then personally introduce you to His Father. Revelation 3:12 says:

> *"He that overcometh will I make a pillar in the temple of my God, and he shall go no more out: and I will write upon him the name of my God, and the name of the city of my God, which is new Jerusalem, which cometh down out of heaven from my God: and I will write upon him my new name."*

God said some people would be pillars in His house. This is another way of saying some people will be presidents, governors, and council chairmen while some of us will be with Him in Jerusalem we will be His senators. We will have several titles, as listed above. The greatest overcomers will be given titles. In Revelation 3:21, we have another reward:

"To him that overcometh will I grant to sit with me in my throne, even as I also overcame, and am set down with my Father in his throne."

Some of us will sit on the same throne on which Jesus Christ is sitting! More than all this, we will be married to Him, according to Revelation 19:5-9:

"And a voice came out of the throne, saying, Praise our God, all ye his servants, and ye that fear him, both small and great. And I heard as it were the voice of a great multitude, and as the voice of many waters, and as the voice of mighty thunderings, saying, Alleluia: for the Lord God omnipotent reigneth. Let us be glad and rejoice, and give honour to him: for the marriage of the Lamb is come, and his wife hath made herself ready. And to her was granted that she should be arrayed in fine linen, clean and white: for the fine linen is the righteousness of saints. And he saith unto me, Write, Blessed are they which are called unto the marriage supper of the Lamb. And he saith unto me, These are the true sayings of God."

The Bible says those who are invited to the wedding are blessed people. What about the bride then? How are you going to describe her blessing? Call on the Lord to help you become an overcomer. If you are not yet bornagain, the best way to begin to overcome is to give your life to Jesus Christ. The best things in this world cannot be compared with the rewards that are waiting for overcomers. All the money in this world cannot buy any fruit from the tree of life. How glorious will it be to sit with God on His throne!

Chapter 13

———◆———

GETTING TO THE TOP

1 Samuel 17:31-37:

"And when the words were heard which David spake, they rehearsed them before Saul: and he sent for him. And David said to Saul, Let no man's heart fail because of him; thy servant will go and fight with this Philistine. And Saul said to David, Thou art not able to go against this Philistine to fight with him: for thou art but a youth, and he a man of war from his youth. And David said unto Saul, Thy servant kept his father's sheep, and there came a lion, and a bear, and took a lamb out of the flock: And I went out after him, and smote him, and delivered it out of his mouth: and when he arose against me, I caught him by his beard, and smote him, and slew him. Thy servant slew both the lion and the bear: and this uncircumcised Philistine shall be as one of them, seeing he hath defied the armies of the living God. David said moreover, The LORD that delivered me out of the paw of the lion, and out of the paw of the bear, he will deliver me out of the hand of this Philistine. And Saul said unto David, Go, and the LORD be with thee."

IT TAKES DILIGENCE TO MAKE IT TO THE TOP

From the passage above, two things are striking, one is that in the army, David was an unknown man, yet within a very short period of joining the army, he was already standing before King Saul. Proverbs 22:29 says:

> *"Seest thou a man diligent in his business? He shall stand before kings; he shall not stand before mean men."*

If David had not been a diligent person, when his brother rebuked him, he would have been discouraged and never would have stood before King Saul. He would never have been there to represent the nation of Israel against the enemy. There are many of us who retire after praying for five minutes. You do not get miracles this way. There are students who study for a short while and think they already know it all. No wonder they keep on failing. Some people become discouraged after failing an examination once or twice and say God did not want them to pass. Our God is a God of success. His plans do not include failure.

If David had not been diligent, he would have ended up with Eliab. He would have become one of the ordinary soldiers. To make it to the top, you have to be diligent. You need to apply yourself to the things of God if Almighty God is to take you where you ought to be.

You need to be in the presence of the King to hear the King. If David was not brought before King Saul, he would not have held any conversation with King Saul. Many of us want to hear God speak but He cannot speak to us if we are too far away. If He wants to talk to us, He will do so through His words. The first time you begin to hear from God. He will use His words to encourage you.

When you say that you are hearing from God, you have to be careful from whom you are hearing because you may be hearing from the devil. The devil can masquerade as the angel of light. When God knows that you have studied His words and you are saturated with them, then He can then begin to talk to you because He knows that you will check whatever He tells you against His unchanging words. Proverbs 10:4 says:

"He becometh poor that dealeth with a slack hand: but the hand of the diligent maketh rich."

If you work hard, you will be made rich. In Proverbs 13:4, the Bible says:

"The soul of the sluggard desireth, and hath nothing: but the soul of the diligent shall be made fat"

The soul of the diligent shall be made fat. It did not say the body of the diligent would be made fat because being fat does not necessarily mean being rich. If you eat unhealthy food, you will be fat. As a matter of fact, God wants you to be slim. The body should be slim while the soul should be fat so that your soul will be filled with the word of God and saturated with the life-giving force that it contains. Proverbs 21:5 says:

"The thoughts of the diligent tend only to plenteousness; but of everyone that is hasty only to want."

If you are hard working, there is no doubt question that, God will reward you. God does not bless the lazy. If you have failed as a carpenter, you are not likely to succeed as a Pastor. If you cannot work with wood successfully, how will you work successfully with human beings? You must be diligent to be a successful. God has no use for the lazy. Romans 12:6-8 says:

"Having then gifts differing according to the grace that is given to us, whether prophecy, let us prophesy according to the proportion of faith; Or ministry, let us wait on our ministering: or he that teacheth, on teaching; Or he that exhorteth, on exhortation: he that giveth, let him do it with simplicity; he that ruleth, with diligence; he that sheweth mercy, with cheerfulness."

It takes diligence to get to the top and it takes diligence to remain there. The problem with many people, particularly in our country, is that they work hard to get to the top and when they get there, they relax. You need to work twice as hard to remain on top than you did to get there. This is true in both the secular and in the spiritual realms. When many of us are new converts, we are diligent, but as we mature spiritually, we relax. To remain where you are, you have to keep running. If you do not keep on moving, those who are behind you will catch up with you and eventually overtake you. Most importantly, you have to be diligent to make it to Heaven. 2 Peter 3:13-14 says:

"Nevertheless we, according to his promise, look for new heavens and a new earth, wherein dwelleth righteousness. Wherefore, beloved, seeing that ye look for such things, be diligent that ye may be found of him in peace, without spot, and blameless."

God has promised us new heavens and a new earth, where we will reign with Him. Even though we have this promise, we have to be diligent to be found in Him in peace, without spots or blemishes. We are saved by grace but the Bible also says we should work out our salvation with fear and trembling. Even after He has given you your salvation, there are things you must do so to ensure the salvation does not slip out of your hands. Even when someone bring a prophecy concerning you, you will still have to work diligently for it.

If you do not want to die in poverty and as a failure, you must be diligent. You can begin your diligence with prayer and in your study the word of God.

OUR GOD CAN REPEAT MIRACLES

David said that the God that delivered him from a lion and a bear would also deliver him from Goliath. What David was saying was that the God who had done something for him in the past would do it again. He had previously delivered him from death and would do so again. When you go through the Bible, you will discover that our God can always repeat miracles. For example, in Exodus 14:14, Moses said to the Israelites that the Lord would fight for them and sure enough, by verse 30, the Lord had fought for them. Not a single one of their enemies remained alive.

In Exodus 17, a different kind of enemy came against the Israelites. The first enemy was Pharaoh and his chariots while the second one was Amalek. In Exodus 17:8-14, we see that the God that fought for them at the Red Sea and gave them victory there, fought for them again. Not only did He destroy their enemies, He even promised that the children and wives of the enemy, who had not come to war, would be destroyed. He said He would wipe out their remembrance. Years later, King Saul was given an assignment, to destroy the Amalekites. This was the fulfilment of the promise.

In 2 Kings 2:8, we find Elijah and Elisha, about to cross the River Jordan. There was no bridge or boat for them to use, so Elijah then took his mantle and smote the River Jordan and the river parted into two. The two of them passed over on dry ground. After Elijah was taken to Heaven, and his mantle fell from his shoulders, Elisha took the mantle. He came back to the river on his way back (2 Kings 2:13-14) and he too smote the river, saying "where is the Lord God of Elijah?" In other words, he was calling on the God that parted the waters earlier to do so a second time, and God answered.

Maybe God has opened a way for you before and right now it seems the way has been blocked, and you do not even know whether to go forward or backward, I have good news for you. The God that opened a way for you before will do so again.

In 2 Kings 5:9-14, we read of Naaman who God cleansed from leprosy. In Matthew 8:1-3, there is an account of a leper who came to Jesus, saying he knew Jesus could make him clean because he knew God can repeat miracles. Jesus cleansed him. If you have an illness that no man can cure, I can assure you, because God has healed others, He will do it for you.

In 2 Kings 6:17, God opened the eyes of the servant of Elisha. In John 9:1-7, Jesus opened the eyes of a man who was born blind. In other words, what He has done before, He can do again. This means if you have problems with your eyes, and you believe God for new eyes, you will get them.

Maybe the problem is that you cannot see the way forward. Many a time, the miracle you need is right by your side but you cannot just see it, like the widow of the son of the prophet. Her creditors were worrying her and she did not know that there was a container of oil in her house that would be the means that God was going to use to perform a miracle. God had to open her eyes to see this. For some of us, our miracle may be in our bedroom right now or in our kitchen, I pray that God will open your eyes to see it.

In 1 Kings 17:17-23, God raised the dead through Elijah. In John 11:39-44, Jesus raised Lazarus from the dead. In other words, He raised the dead earlier and He did it again. Because He has done it several times already, there is no reason why He cannot do it again. If your business is dead, it can come alive today. If your marriage is dead, it can come back to life again. If your brain is dead, God can give you a brand new brain. In Hebrews 13:8, the Bible talks of:

> *"Jesus Christ the same yesterday, and today, and forever."* while Malachi 3:6 says:

> *"For I am the LORD, I change not; therefore ye sons of Jacob are not consumed."*

If you can remember one problem that God had solved for you before, I can assure you that you will soon have a new testimony of another problem solved.

Only a Good Shepherd will make a Good King

David was an excellent shepherd boy. He never ran back to his father when he was faced with the lion and the bear. He destroyed both of them so as to protect of the sheep kept in his care. David risked his life. The Bible says in John 10:11, when Jesus was talking about shepherds:

> *"I am the good shepherd: the good shepherd giveth his life for the sheep."*

If you have ever won a single soul to Christ, then you are a shepherd.

All your converts are your sheep and God expects you to give your life for your sheep. Your life is made up of your time, energy, money, contacts and all your abilities, rolled together. You are supposed to use all these gifts to make sure that your converts will stand. You must make sure that they do not backslide. If you really take care of your converts, even if they go away for ten years, they will come back home. If they do not come back home, it means that when they were at home, you did not make home habitable for them.

Jesus gave His life for us and that is why He was given a Name that is above every other name, according to Philippians 2:8-10. God made a promise to every one of us in Revelation 2:10:

> *"Fear none of those things which thou shall suffer: behold, the devil shall cast some of you into prison, that ye may be tried; and ye shall have tribulation ten days: be thou faithful unto death, and I will give thee a crown of life."*

If you can be faithful unto death as David and Jesus Christ were, you will receive a crown of life. David became a king because he was a good shepherd. Be a good shepherd and you will wear the crown of life.

David grabbed the lion by the beard, and all of a sudden, supernatural strength came into his hands. God is not asking you to be strong in your own strength. He says that you should be strong in the Lord and in the power of His might (Ephesians 6:10). All that He is requiring from you is that you be courageous and brave the battle, He will supply the strength. God told Joshua in Joshua 1:9 to be strong and courageous and He would be with him. Also, In Isaiah 26:4, the Bible says:

> *"Trust ye in the LORD forever: for in the LORD JEHOVAH is everlasting strength:"*

There is strength in the Lord. There is power in the Lord. There is victory in the Lord. If you stand in Him, and He will give you victory.

Chapter 14

TWO SONGS

1 Samuel 17:33-37:

> *"And Saul said to David, Thou art not able to go against this Philistine to fight with him: for thou art but a youth and he a man of war from his youth. And David said unto Saul, Thy servant kept his father's sheep, and there came a lion, and a bear, and took a lamb out of the flock: And I went out after him, and smote him, and delivered it out of his mouth: and when he arose against me, I caught him by his beard, and smote him, and slew him. Thy servant slew both the lion and the bear: and this uncircumcised Philistine shall be as one of them, seeing he hath defied the armies of the living God. David said moreover, The LORD that delivered me out of the paw of the lion, and out of the paw of the bear, he will deliver me out of the hand of this Philistine. And Saul said unto David, Go and the LORD be with thee."*

THE SONG OF A BACKSLIDER

A backslider is recognised by his speech. When you listen to the vocabulary of someone who is no longer with God, you will know very quickly that they are a backslider. King Saul had become a backslider. God rejected him. When Goliath appeared tall as he was, he could not stand before him. He felt everybody must feel the same. He felt nobody could face Goliath if he could not face him. This is the language of a backslider.

In Numbers 13:31-33, we read is the account of the ten spies. When they came back from the land flowing with milk and honey, they said the land was good. However they said they could not take the land because there were giants in the land who would destroy them. Backsliders always think negatively. There are people who believe that it is impossible to have divine health all the days of one's life. I am not one of them. There are some that do not believe that God can supply all their needs. I do not belong to this group.

In Numbers 14:1-4, as a result of what the ten spies said, the children of Israel talked of electing a captain and going back to Egypt. This shows clearly that God was no longer with them. Whenever you hear someone saying, "if it is not possible to go forward let us go back," you should know that you are talking to a backslider. When someone tells you that if prayer cannot solve the problem you should use witchcraft, you can be sure a backslider is talking to you.

In Joshua 7:10-12, after Israel had been defeated at Ai and Joshua had fallen on his face and cried out to God, God told him that the cause of their defeat was because they had sinned. God had departed from them. Whenever you find somebody who is running away from the enemy, you can be sure that this person is a backslider. Any time somebody begins to tell you to take it easy, or and that your enemies are strong, you can be sure that the person talking to you is a backslider. Jesus said in John 15:5:

> *"I am the vine, ye are the branches: He that abideth in me, and I him, the same bringeth forth much fruit: for without me ye can do nothing."*

Judges 16:20 provides a particularly tragic example in Samson. When he lost contact with God, he could not defeat the enemy. The Bible says he did not know that God had departed from him. You must stay away from anything that may anger God. The more you see His miracles in your life, the closer you must draw to Him. The more He demonstrates His power in your life, the more you must make sure you do not do anything to offend Him. In separating yourself from Him, you will discover that you will become powerless.

THE SONG OF THE STEADFAST

The song of the steadfast is always characterised by phrases such as, 'I can do it' 'It is possible', 'There is hope' and so on. While the ten spies said they could not, Numbers 13:30 records Caleb's response:

"And Caleb stilled the people before Moses, and said, Let us go up at once, and possess it; for we are well able to overcome it."

In Numbers 14:9, Caleb and Joshua also said:

"Only rebel not ye against the LORD, neither fear ye the people of the land; for they are bread for us: their defence is departed from them, and the LORD is with us: fear them not."

In Numbers 14:24, God said concerning Caleb:

"But my servant Caleb, because he had another spirit with him, and hath followed me fully, him will I bring into the land whereinto he went; and his seed shall possess it."

Caleb followed God fully and therefore he could say they were able to possess the land. I know I am able. I know that with God on my side, there is no mountain I cannot climb and there is no goal I cannot reach. Whenever you begin to hear a man say that a problem will soon become a testimony, you can be sure that the man is walking closely with God. Zechariah 4:6-7 says:

"The he answered and spake unto me, saying, This is the word of the LORD unto Zerubbabel, saying, Not by might nor by power, but by my spirit, saith the LORD of hosts. Who art thou, O great mountain? before Zerubbabel thou shalt become a plain: and he shall bring forth the headstone thereof with shoutings, crying, Grace, grace unto it."

When a man is in contact with God he sees problems as stepping stones to testimonies. Everyone who is closely linked to God should be able to say as Paul said in Philippians 4:13:

"I can do all things through Christ, which strengtheneth me."

Paul also said in Philippians 4:19:

"But my God shall supply all your need according to his riches in glory by Christ Jesus."

Why do you find those who are close to God so bold and singing the song of victory in the face of trouble? Why do you find people who are so bold telling Nebuchadnezzar that they will go into the fire and that their God will deliver them? It is because, according to Ephesians 6:10, their strength is in the Lord. They do not look at themselves but at God. How much you achieve is determined by how great your view is of God. Shadrach, Meshach and Abednego said their God was able to deliver them and that He would deliver them (Daniel 3:17). David told Saul that his God who had delivered him from a lion and a bear would deliver him as he faced Goliath. Luke 1:37 says:

"For with God nothing shall be impossible."

In Matthew 14:23-29, Jesus was walking on water and Peter asked if he could join Him. The Lord told him to come, and he jumped out of the boat and walked on the water to meet Jesus. The moment he doubted, he began to sink. However, he was already walking on water. This should have been enough to convince him that with God are all things possible. Jesus said in Mark 9:23:

"If thou canst believe, all things are possible to him that believeth."

If only you believe, all things will be possible for you. When you believe, you have a link with the One who can do all things, and when you have a link with the One who can do all things, He will do all things through you. You may not feel able to do all things, but when you are linked with the Rock of Ages, everything becomes possible for you.

Chapter 15

OUR WEAPONS ARE NOT CARNAL

1 Samuel 17:38-40

"And Saul armed David with his armour, and he put an helmet of brass upon his head; also he armed him with a coat of mail, And David girded his sword upon his armour, and he assayed to go; for he had not proved it. And David said unto Saul, I cannot go with these; for I have not proved them, And David put them off him. And he took his staff in his hand, and chose him five smooth stones out of the brook, and put them in a shepherd's bag which he had, even in a scrip; and his sling was in his hand: and he drew near to the Philistine."

Saul could not go and fight Goliath, and when he saw that David was determined to go, he wanted to share part of the glory just in case David was successful. He told David to wear his armour. David put it on and it was very heavy and awkward so he discarded it. When David got to the brook, he chose five smooth stones. When you want to fight a spiritual battle, you cannot use physical weapons. In 2 Corinthians 10:4, the Bible says the weapons of our warfare are not carnal. I have seen people pray prayers that make me laugh. They kick and shout as they pray, saying they are kicking the devil physically.

You cannot kick the devil physically. People who say t fight the devil are wasting their time, as are those v. against the devil. Psalm 20:7-8 says:

"Some trust in chariots, and some in horses: but we will remem̶ name of the LORD our God. They are brought down and fallen: but we aᵣ̶ risen, and stand upright."

Those who put their trust in horses and chariots stumble and fall while we stand. You cannot fight the devil with the weapons of the world. You cannot win a spiritual battle by riding in a chariot Christians win battles on their knees. A man who is on his knees is far more powerful than a man armed with all the machine guns in the world.

Jeremiah 17:5 makes it clear that you are already cursed if you put your trust in human beings. However, when you put your trust in the Almighty God, you are blessed. God, unlike men, will not fail you. He is the only one available all the time. You do not need an appointment to speak to God. You just need to focus on God. Hebrews 12:2 says:

"Looking unto Jesus the author and finisher of our faith; who for the joy that was set before him endured the cross, despising the shame, and is set down at the right hand of the throne of God."

Ephesians 6:10-18 tells us to be strong in the Lord and in the power of His might and put on the whole armour of God. Not the whole armour of your Pastor or the whole armour of any organisation. The whole armour of God is Jesus. Once you are protected by Jesus, you are more than a conqueror. This is why Paul said in Philippians 4:13 that he could do all things through Christ who strengthens him. You do not need any other weapon apart from Jesus Christ.

FIVE SMOOTH STONES

David picked up five smooth stones. Not five ordinary stones. Not five rough stones. Anyone that God will use must not be an ordinary stone but a smooth one. It is not enough for you to be a Christian. You must be an exceptionally pure and holy Christian. God only uses smooth stones. Leviticus 10:8-10 says:

"And the LORD spake unto Aaron, saying, Do not drink wine nor strong drink, thou, nor thy sons with thee, when ye go into the tabernacle of the congregation, lest ye die: it shall be a statute for ever throughout your generations: And that ye may put difference between holy and unholy, and between unclean and clean;"

This command was for Aaron and his children and not for the whole congregation, because Aaron and his children were consecrated to God. If you want to be only ordinary Christian, you do not need to bother with all these details. However, if you want to be a battleaxe in the hand of Almighty God, and a terror to the enemy, like Aaron and his sons, you must go a step further. This will result in you no longer being an ordinary stone but a smooth one. In Daniel 1:8-16 the Bible tells us of Daniel, Meshach, Shadrach and Abednego, who were among the first group of Israelites taken into captivity in Babylon. When they got there, the king selected them for special treatment – good food, wine, and training – but they refused. They decided not to defile themselves with the meat and wine of the king, which would have been offered to an idol. They preferred to eat beans and water.

It is interesting that later on, when Shadrach, Meshach and Abednego were thrown into the fiery furnace, the fire did not burn them, because they were special children. It is noteworthy that when they threw Daniel into the lion's den, the lions did not eat him because he was a smooth stone.

Joseph refused the advances of the wife of Potiphar because he was a smooth stone. He said he could not compromise and sin against God. As a result of this, he landed up in prison but God had planned that he would arrive at the throne through the prison. Paul said in 1 Corinthians 9:25-27:

"And every man that striveth for the mastery is temperate in all things. Now they do it to obtain a corruptible crown; but we an incorruptible. I therefore so run, not as uncertainly; so fight I, not as one that beateth the air: but I keep under my body, and bring it into subjection: lest that by any means, when I have preached to others, I myself should be castaway."

The Bible says in Colossians 3:5-6:

"Mortify therefore your members which are upon the earth; fornication,

uncleanness, inordinate affections, evil concupiscence, and covetousness, which is idolatry: For which things' sake the wrath of God cometh on the children of disobedience:"

Mortify your body. You should be able to control all parts of your body. Hebrew 1:9 tells us clearly that anyone who wants to operate under the anointing of the most High God must not only love righteousness, but must hate iniquity. He must not just be holy; he must be thoroughly pure. Jeremiah 15:19-21 says:

"Therefore thus saith the LORD, If thou return, then will I bring thee again, and thou shalt stand before me: and if thou take forth the precious from the vile, thou shalt be as my mouth: let them return unto thee; but return not thou unto them. And I will make thee unto this people a fenced brasen wall: and they shall fight against thee, but they shall not prevail against thee: for I am with thee to save thee and to deliver thee, saith the LORD. And I will deliver thee out of the hand of the wicked, and I will redeem thee out of the hand of the terrible."

You must separate the pure from the impure. You must become a smooth stone to deal with the Goliaths of this world for if you discipline yourself, your enemies will fall before you. This is the promise of God. Malachi 3:3 says:

"And he shall sit as a refiner and purifier of silver: and he shall purify the sons of Levi, and purge them as gold and silver, that they may offer unto the LORD an offering in righteousness."

How will you become a smooth stone? The Almighty God can help you by passing you through fire. In Zechariah 13:8-9, He says He will refine the remnant with fire – the refining we are talking about is not for everybody but for the remnant. If God is interested in you and wants to use you for His glory. He will make you smooth. He will do it by fire. He can use the fire of affliction, by creating problems for you until you submit.

He can also use the fire of the Holy Spirit that will burn away the dross and leave you pure and smooth and a vessel unto honour. The choice is yours: do you want to be made smooth?

Chapter 16

———◆◆◆———

NEVER UNDERESTIMATE YOUR ENEMY

1 Samuel 17:41-43

"And the Philistine came on and drew near unto David; and the man that bare the shield went before him. And when the Philistine looked about, and saw David, he disdained him: for he was but a youth, and ruddy, and of a fair countenance. And the Philistine said unto David, Am I a dog that thou comest to me with staves? And the Philistine cursed David by his gods."

When Goliath saw David, he disdained him. He was shocked that someone with no sword had come to fight him. He asked; 'Am I a dog?'

DO NOT UNDERESTIMATE YOUR ENEMY

The first lesson we have to learn here, is that as Christians, we must never underestimate our enemies. A small snake can be full of deadly poison. The Bible tells us in Matthew 26:41 to watch and pray so that we do not fall into temptation. The Bible tells us in 1 Peter 5:8 to be sober and be vigilant because our adversary, the devil, is walking about like a roaring lion, looking for whom to devour.

In Joshua 7:2-6, the Bible tells us that after the fall of Jericho, Joshua thought that having taken Jericho, the city of Ai would pose no problems. He underestimated and lost thirty six men. Ai was small but Satan had already entered into Achan and encouraged him to steal something from God. As a result of this, God left the children of Israel and unfortunately, Joshua did not immediately go back to God for instructions.

Anybody who becomes overconfident will fall. Take heed lest you fall. In Judges 16:6-21, we discover that it was over confidence that destroyed Samson. Delilah asked him repeatedly about the secret of his strength and how he could be captured. Samson should have recognised the danger he was in, but he underestimated Delilah and fell. Many of us have one little enemy – a little anger occasionally which we think we can handle. Moses became angry only once in forty years but as a result, he did not make it into the promised land. You must not underestimate your enemy. The Bible tells us in the Song of Songs 2:15 that we should beware of little foxes. These are things we think are not very important, but they can be the most dangerous of all, Look at Proverbs 6:10-11:

"Yet a little sleep, a little slumber, a little folding of the hands to sleep: So shall thy poverty come as one that travelleth, and thy want as an armed man."

Sleep here refers not just to physical sleep but also to spiritual sleep. Just a little slumber and this leads to sleep. Your three-hour prayer session reduces to two hours and then to one hour. Before you know it you have fallen.

The Almighty God expects His children to be on fire all the time. In 1 Thessalonians 5:16-17, the Bible says we should rejoice evermore but pray without ceasing. The Bible says that when you have done all things you are to stand, (Ephesians 6:13). Remain constantly on fire. The price of liberty is unending vigilance. Do not underestimate your enemy. When you have won a victory, stand and prepare for the next battle.

WHO IS A DOG?

Goliath asked David a very serious question, 'Am I a dog?' This is a very pertinent question. We as Christians ought to know who exactly is a dog, from God's point of view. We will find out from the Bible. Revelation 22:15 says:

"For without are dogs, and sorcerers, and whoremongers, and murderers, and idolaters, and whosoever loveth and maketh a lie."

Dogs are those who will never enter Heaven, no matter what they do. They are people who will be outside when God shuts the gate of Heaven. Those who are in this category are mentioned in the Bible verse above. We discover more about them in? Proverbs 26:11:

"As a dog returneth to his vomit, so a fool returneth to his folly." Peter 2:20-22 provides some further detail:

"For if after they have escaped the pollutions of the world through the knowledge of the Lord and Saviour Jesus Christ, they are again entangled therein, and overcome, the latter end is worse with them than the beginning. For it had been better for them not to have known the way of righteousness, than after they have known it, to turn from the holy commandment delivered unto them. But it is happened unto them according to the true proverb. The dogs turned to his own vomit again; and the sow that was washed to her wallowing in the more."

There are also dogs that have never known Christ, according to Matthew 15:25-26. Here Jesus Christ said He could not give the bread of children to dogs. There are two classes of people: children and dogs. Children are those who do the will of their Father. They are living holy lives. Dogs are those who enjoy sin. Psalm 22:16 calls wicked people dogs. Matthew 7:6 warns us not to give holy things to dogs. Dogs do not value holy things. They are not interested in fasting, prayer, Bible study, self-sacrifice and spiritual development.

In Deuteronomy 23:18, a prostitute is compared to a dog. If you are an adulterer or a fornicator, you are a dog and you must do something about it. 2 Kings 8:12-13 shows that a dog is somebody who is capable of doing any form of evil:

"And Hazael said, Why weepeth my lord? And he answered, Because I know the evil that thou wilt do unto the children of Israel: their strong holds

wilt thou set on fire, and their young men wilt thou slay with the sword, and wilt dash their children and rip up their women with child.And Hazael said, But what, is thy servant a dog, that he should do this great thing? And Elisha answered, The LORD hath shewed me that thou shalt be king over Syria."

It is only a dog who can rip open a woman who is pregnant with child. It is only a dog who can dash the head of a little child against the wall. A backslider is a dangerous person because as a dog, he can do any evil. Samuel said Saul would kill him if he discovered that he had gone to anoint somebody else as king. This shows how far he had sunk, if he was capable of committing murder.

In Philippians 3:2 the Bible says we should beware of dogs. Beware of backsliders. You should also pray that you do not backslide. The gate of Heaven is permanently shut against dogs. If you know that you are already a backslider, you desperately need to run back to God and ask for His mercy. Leave your kennel and return to your life as a son. If you are already a son, ask God to keep you growing higher.

Chapter 17

---◆---

ON CURSES AND BLESSINGS

1 Samuel 17:43:

> *"And the Philistine said unto David, Am I a dog that thou comest to me with staves? And the Philistine cursed David by his gods."*

THE CURSE WITH NO CAUSE SHALL NOT COME TO PASS.

Goliath cursed David. A curse is a very powerful weapon. It is an invitation to supernatural forces to attack your enemy. Goliath cursed David by his gods. He invited his gods to come and help him fight against David. In Numbers 22:2-6 we read of a king inviting a prophet to come and curse the children of Israel. However, just as it is written in Proverbs 26:2, the curse did not come to pass as there was no reason for it:

> *"As the bird by wandering as the swallow by flying, so the curse causeless shall not come."*

If I have not offended you and you curse me, you are wasting your time. When any Christian is on the side of the Lord, anybody trying to put a charm on them is wasting his time, according to Numbers 23:23:

"Surely there is no enchantment against Jacob, neither is there any divination against Israel: according to this time it shall be said of Jacob and of Israel, What hath God wrought!"

Also Numbers 22:12 says:

"And God said unto Balaam, Thou shalt not go with them; thou shalt not curse the people: for they are blessed."

When you are on the side of the Lord, you are blessed. In Numbers 23:8, Balaam confirms that if you are blessed, no curse can have effect on you:

"How shall I curse, whom God hath not cursed? Or how shall I defy, whom the LORD hath not defied?"

If you are on the Lord's side, according to Genesis 12:1-3, God will curse anybody that curses you. This was the promise of God to Abraham.

However, there are certain curses that are settled. Nobody needs to pronounce these curses before they work, In Proverbs 17:13, we have one of them:

"Whoso rewardeth evil for good, evil shall not depart from his house."

Anyone who rewards evil for good should prepare for trouble. Another person who is also already cursed is someone who is barren - in other words, anybody. This is somebody who does not bear fruit for God. Look at John 15:1-2:

"I am the true vine, and my Father is the husbandman. Every branch in me that beareth not fruit he taketh away: and every branch that beareth fruit, he purgeth it, that it may bring forth more fruit."

Here we have a powerful statement. It is a warning that Almighty God will bear the nominal believer away from Christ. You must witness on that basis. You must win souls so that this curse will not come on you.

BLESSINGS BASELESS SHALL NOT BE

For a blessing to be effective there must be a reason for it. A blessing is an invitation to supernatural powers to assist support and exalt somebody that you love. In Genesis 27:1-4, we have the principle behind blessing. Isaac told Esau to do something pleasing to him so that he would bless him. If you desire God's blessings, you must obey him. Please Him and He will bless you.

Deuteronomy 28:1-13 is a passage that is a great encouragement for a Christian. It talks about many good things. However, many of us overlook the basis for all the blessings in the passage. The basis is written in verse 1:

> *"And it shall come to pass, if thou shalt hearken diligently unto the voice of the LORD thy God, to observe and to do all his commandments which I command thee this day, that the LORD thy God will set thee on high above all nations of the earth:"*

The one who obey all God's commandments of God will please Him. When God is pleased, He will bless you.

In Malachi 3:10 God said that if we bring all the tithes into His house. He would open the windows of Heaven and pour out so great a blessing on us that there would not be enough room to receive it. God is always asking us to do something to please Him so that He can open the windows of heaven and pour down blessings on us.

In Luke 5:1-11, God asked Peter for the use of his boat. It was after Peter surrendered his boat and Jesus used the boat to preach that He decided to bless him in return. In 1 Kings 17:8-16 when Elijah came to the widow of Zarepath and the woman said she had only one meal left, the man of God insisted that he be fed first before he could pronounce a blessing on her. Everybody has to do something in order to open the doors for blessings.

In 2 Kings 4:8-17 we find the story of the Shunamite woman. Elisha was passing by one day when this woman invited him to come and eat in her house every time he was in Shunem. She also provided accommodation for him. After some time, Elisha blessed her. This is one place in the Bible where somebody who did not believe got a miracle. The woman did not believe the prophecy of Elisha that she would have a baby. However, because what Elisha said was a blessing and not a prayer, it came to pass. Proverbs 11:25 says:

"The liberal soul shall be made fat: and he that watereth shall be watered also himself."

It is your actions you do where will bring blessings to you. In Genesis 22:15-18 after Abraham had surrendered Isaac to God, God said that by Himself He swore that He would bless and multiply Abraham's seed. When you make God extremely happy, He will pronounce a blessing on you that nobody can ever change. When you give Him your best, he will give you His best.

In Philippians 3:7-11, Paul said he had surrendered everything that was import to him so that he may win Christ of God. In Acts 19:11-12 we are told that Paul's handkerchief cast out demons. The sweat of Paul with which it was impregnated contained power. This blessing came from God because of Paul's service to Him. You must make haste to do what God requires if you desire the blessing of God on your life. In Genesis 27:3-33 when Esau returned from hunting and brought what his father had asked for, it was too late. The glorious blessing of the first born had been given to somebody else.

What will you choose? A curse or a blessing? If you are already a believer, if there are areas of your life where you have been making God angry, repent. If you have been holding back from doing certain things that God has been telling you to do, repent. Then from the bottom of your heart, think of some things that you can do please God and begin to do them at once.

If you are not yet saved, you cannot ask for the blessings of God. Anyone who is living in sin is an enemy of God. God cannot bless His enemy. You must address your enmity with God now.

Chapter 18

OVERCONFIDENCE AND PRIDE

1 Samuel 7:44-47:

> "And the Philistine said to David, Come to me, and I will give thy flesh unto
> the fowls of the air, and to the beasts of the field. Then said David to the
> Philistine, Thou comest to me with a sword, and with a spear, and with a
> shield: but I come to thee in the name of the LORD of hosts, the God of the
> armies of Israel, whom thou hast defied. This day will the LORD deliver thee
> into mine hand; and I will smite thee, and take thine head from thee; and
> I will give the carcasses of the host of the Philistines this day unto the fowls
> of the air, and to the wild beasts of the earth; that all the earth may know
> that there is a God in Israel. And all this assembly shall know that the LORD
> saveth not with sword and spear: for the battle is the LORD's and he will
> give you into our hands."

Goliath came to the battle with a sword and a spear while David came in the
name of the Lord of hosts. One boasted of his own might while the other
boasted that the Lord would win the victory.

OVERCONFIDENCE AND PRIDE ARE TWO DANGEROUS RELATIVES

Goliath was overconfident. He never thought David could come near him, let alone defeat him. Before the fight, he thought that he had already won. We must beware of overconfidence. Many people have failed because they become overconfident. For intellectuals this is a particular danger. If overconfidence is dangerous in the natural realm, it is even more dangerous in the spiritual. Many of us boast that nothing can stop us from getting to Heaven and we relax and become overconfident. The Bible says in 1 Corinthians 10:12:

"Wherefore let him that thinketh he standeth take heed lest he fall."

The standing position is the most dangerous position of all. If you do not remember that you are only standing thanks to the power of God, then you are in danger. In 1 Peter 1:5, the Bible makes it clear that we are kept by the power of God. In Luke 22:31:34 we can learn a lesson that many of us easily overlook:

"And the Lord said, Simon, Simon, behold, Satan hath desired to have you, that he may sift you as wheat: But I have prayed for thee, that thy faith fail not: and when thou art converted, strengthen thy brethren. And he said unto him, Lord, I am ready to go with thee, both into prison, and to death. And he said, I tell thee, Peter, the cock shall not crow this day, before that thou shalt thrice deny that thou knowest me."

Here the Lord told Peter that the devil wanted to use him but He had prayed for him and that afterwards, he should strengthen his brethren. Peter had said that he would never deny Jesus, and that he was ready to die with Him. The Lord then changed his tone and asserted that Peter would deny Him three times that same day. Peter was overconfident and he fell. Overconfidence can destroy. This was what destroyed Samson (Judges 16:6-17). It was the reason why Joshua failed to capture Ai (Joshua 7:2-5. In James 4:13-15, the Bible says:

"Go to now, ye that say, To day or to morrow we will go into such a city, and continue there a year, and buy and sell, and get gain: Whereas ye know not what shall be on the morrow, For what is your life? It is even a vapour, that appeareth for a little time, and then vanisheth away. For that ye ought to say, If the Lord will, we shall live, and do this, or that."

Do not boast about what you will do tomorrow. You are not in control of tomorrow. Only God controls tomorrow. Every child of God must always say, 'If God wills'.

Overconfidence is what leads to pride. When you are too confident about yourself, you feel you do not need God. God says in Proverbs 6:16-19:

> *"These six things doth the LORD hate; yea, seven are an abomination unto him: A proud look, a lying tongue, and hands that shed innocent blood, An heart that deviseth wicked imaginations, feet that be swift in running to mischief, A false witness that speaketh lies, and he that soweth discord among brethren."*

Top of the list of things that are an abomination to God is pride. Somebody, who commits murder, as far as God is concerned, is less evil than someone who is proud. In James 4:6, the Bible warns:

> *"But he giveth more grace. Wherefore he saith, God resisteth the proud, but giveth grace unto the humble."*

I pray that God will not resist you. Goliath was overconfident, became proud and this led to his destruction.

LET GOD FIGHT YOUR BATTLES

David's speech made it clear that he was not the one to fight the battle. He said he was the representative of the Lord of Hosts and that He would hand over his enemy to Him. He was aware that on his own, he could not win the battle. He was also aware that with God on his side, victory was sure. Many of us have been fighting and we have been losing simply because we have been fighting our battles by ourselves. If only you will let God fight your battles, not only will you win; you will not suffer any injury in the process.

There are certain things that God can do that you cannot do. We know from Exodus 14:13-28 that God can divide the Red Sea. You cannot do this. He can drown your enemy. You cannot do this. He can swallow up your enemy while you are watching. Why not let Him fight your battles? Joshua 6:1-21 shows how God can destroy your enemy while you are shouting 'alleluia'. It was a shout by the children of Israel that brought the great and impenetrable wall of Jericho crashing down. He can do such things for you too. If you allow Him to fight your battles. He will destroy the defences of your enemies.

In Joshua 10:8-11, when Joshua was fighting against certain kings that were gathered against him, as they were running away, God attacked them from above. God can destroy your enemies while you are sleeping or enjoying yourself. In Numbers 16:23-33, after some people had rebelled against Moses, Moses called to the Lord, and God fought for him. He told him to separate these enemies so He could to deal with them. The ground opened its mouth and swallowed them.

In 2 Chronicles 20:20-25 the Bible tells us that when Jehoshaphat went to fight the three kings that came against him, all he did was praise God and the Lord did the rest. He caused these enemies to destroy each other. He can still do this today. When you praise the Almighty God and He accepts your worship, the result is that your enemies will destroy themselves without you needing to do anything to them. There is nothing that can kill God. In Deuteronomy 32:40, He said:

"For I lift up my hand to heaven, and say, I live forever."

If you let God fight for you, long after your enemies have been defeated, God will still be God. In 1 Kings 8:27, the Bible tells us that the Heavens of Heaven cannot contain God. There is nowhere your enemies can run to escape from God. No man is greater than God, according to Ecclesiastes 5:8. If God be for us who can be against us? (Romans 8:31). Psalm 68:1-3 says:

"Let God arise, let his enemies be scattered: let them also that hate him flee before him. As smoke is driven away, so drive them away: as wax melteth before the fire, so let the wicked perish at the presence of God: But let the righteous be glad; let them rejoice before God: yea, let them exceedingly rejoice."

Before you ask God to arise and fight your battles, first make sure that you are not your own enemy. Make sure you are not an enemy of God. If you are an enemy of God or you are your own enemy, when you call on God to arise, He will arise against you. If you are not a Christian, you are an enemy of God. If you are living in sin, you are an enemy of God. If you love the things of this world rather than God, you are an enemy of God. You must repent – today.

You are your own enemy when you know what God wants you to do and you refuse to do it. When He says you should pray and study the Bible and you refuse, you are your own enemy. When He asks you to witness and you refuse, you become your own enemy. When God gives you instructions and you fail to carry them out, you are your own enemy. You can address this today and then you may ask Him to fight your battles for you.

Chapter 19

---◆◆◆---

GOD WILL PLAY HIS PART

1 Samuel 17:48:

> *"And it came to pass, when the Philistine arose, and came and drew nigh to meet David, that David hasted, and ran toward the army to meet the Philistine."*

As long as your enemy is boasting and not doing anything, you can relax. You can still refer to Psalm 23:5 where David said God prepared a table before him in the presence of his enemies. However, the moment the enemy begins to move, you must do something very quickly.

In 1 Peter 5:8-9, the Bible makes it clear that the enemy is not inactive. The enemy is walking about seeking for whom to devour. You must act quickly. The enemy is already moving. You must move – and move faster than the enemy. The Bible makes it clear to us in Mark 16:17-18 that certain signs shall follow those who believe. If you are not on the move, these signs will not follow you.

David hastened and ran while Goliath rose and began to walk, just like the devil, whom he symbolises. The Bible says the eyes of the Lord run to and fro across the whole earth. The one who is running will arrive faster than the one who is walking. When you move, God will move with you. In Psalm 121:5 the Bible says Almighty God is your shade on your right hand. When you act, God will act with you. When you decide to fight the enemy, the Almighty God will fight with you. In Psalm 68:1-3, the Bible says if God arises, His enemies will scatter. If your enemies have not been scattered, it is most likely that you have not been moving. When the enemy moves an inch, you must move several inches faster. The Bible tells us in James 4:7 that it is when you resist the devil that he will flee. If you do not resist the devil then the devil is not going to flee. It is vital to put pressure on the enemy.

In Judges 14:5-6, the Bible tells us that as Samson was going to Timnath, a lion roared at him. He did not wait for the lion to jump before he grabbed him and tore him in two. Also Joshua 10:6-19 tells us that several kings decided to attack the Gibeonites, who had made peace with Joshua. When they sought help from Joshua, he moved immediately. He came against the enemy suddenly. If you do not attack the enemy suddenly, even though God will give you victory, the enemy can embarrass you a little. There are certain things that you must do. For instance, you must pray. The Bible says we should pray without ceasing. The first thing you have to ask yourself before facing an enemy is whether God is still with you. If God is with you, you will be on the winning side. Once you are sure that the Lord is still with you after you have prayed, the next thing to do is to give thanks. In all things, give thanks (1 Thessalonians 5:18). Thank God that all this time, the enemy has not been able to destroy you and that now you will deal with the enemy.

Another thing that you should do when confronting an enemy is found in Luke 6:38:

> *"Give, and it shall be given unto you; good measure, pressed down, and shaken together, and running over, shall men give into your bosom. For with the same measure that ye mete withal it shall be measured to you again."*

Many of us do not realise the significance of giving when it comes to spiritual warfare. If you pay your tithe, the windows of Heaven will open. God will see you and the angels will pay attention to you. Nobody will be able to harm you in this type of situation. Furthermore, God will open the windows of Heaven and pour down on you abundant blessings.

Chapter 20

PROBLEMS AND SOLUTIONS

1 Samuel 17:48-53:

"And it came to pass, when the Philistine arose, and came and drew nigh to meet David, that David hasted, and ran toward the army to meet the Philistine. And David put his hand in his bag, and took thence a stone, and slang it, and smote the Philistine in his forehead, that the stone sunk into his forehead; and he fell upon his face to the earth. So David prevailed over the Philistine with a sling and with a stone, and smote the Philistine, and slew him; but there was no sword in the hand of David. Therefore David ran, and stood upon the Philistine, and took his sword, and drew it out of the sheath thereof, and slew him, and cut off his head therewith. And when the Philistines saw their champion was dead, they fled. And the men of Israel and of Judah arose, and shouted, and pursued the Philistines, until thou come to the valley, and to the gates of Ekron. And the wounded of the Philistines fell down by the way to Shaaraim, even unto Gath, and unto Ekron."

As the showdown between David and Goliath reach its climax, we can all discover several beautiful pieces of truth.

EVERY GIANT HAS A WEAK SPOT (EVERY PROBLEM HAS A SOLUTION).

In spite of the size of Goliath, and his armour, he had a weak spot. There was one part of his body that was not covered by any armour and this was where the stone from the sling struck him. This caused the downfall of Goliath. Every problem you may encounter will have at least one solution. Locating the weak spot in a giant is a task for every prayer warrior. Apparently, while everybody was looking at the size of Goliath and his armour, David was searching for the weak spot in him and discovered that it was the forehead. He knew that what he needed to do was to aim a stone at that weak spot. When you study this story in detail, you will notice that David moved so quickly that Goliath did not even have the time to pick up his sword. When David wanted to cut of his head, he had to pull the sword out of the sheath first.

Every problem you encounter has a solution. The beauty of it is that the solution is wrapped up in Jesus Christ. Jesus said in John 14:6 that He is the way. He is the way out of every problem. Whatever may be the problem in your life, it has a solution in Jesus. If it is sickness or disease, according to Isaiah 53:5, the Bible says that by His stripes we are healed. If you are sick or diseased, the stone you have to throw at that sickness or disease is the word of God that says by His stripes you are healed. If you hold on to this fact, I can guarantee you that the healing will come.

If you find yourself often falling into sin and you are concerned that you may not make it to Heaven, there is a way out of sin. 1 John 1:7 makes it clear that the blood of Jesus Christ cleanses us from all sins. It does not matter what you have done in the past; His blood will cleanse you from all sins.

Maybe your problem is weakness – emotional, physical, spiritual – there is a way out according to Nehemiah 8:10, which says the joy of the Lord is your strength. If you will learn to rejoice in the Lord regularly, you will be amazed how suddenly your weakness will become strength. If you feel depressed or sad, there is an answer too. This is found in Philippians 4:4 which tells us to rejoice in the Lord always. Because the Lord is always constant, your joy will also be constant.

Suppose you find yourself overwhelmed by all sorts of problems and you feel defeated. There is a way out. Romans 8:28 says all things work together for good to those that love God. So when you find yourself defeated and everything seems to be going wrong, ask yourself whether you still love God. If you do, you can be sure that whatever is happening, even though you may not understand why, is going to end up for your good.

Another important thing to learn from the story of David and Goliath is that when the stone hit Goliath and he fell, David did not stop there. He made sure that he cut off his head so that he could not recover. Once you cut off the head of a man, the contest is over. Do not leave your enemy half-dead. Make sure his head is cut off. Do not just ask God to heal you. Pray that you will enjoy divine health. Do not just pray that God will pay your debt, but that you will never need to borrow again. Do not just pray for a partner but also that you will be received in the home to which you are going.

Also, remember that your greatest enemy is yourself and not the devil. If your body does not co-operate with the devil he will not be able to work. In dealing with your flesh, ensure you do a thorough job. Paul said in Galatians 2:20 that he was crucified with Christ. In 2 Corinthians 5:17 the Bible says that if you are in Christ you are a new creature. If things in your life do not seem new, assess the reality of your salvation. Pray until you know that you are sure you are a new creature. Pray for sanctification and the baptism of the Holy Spirit. Anything that the devil could use in future to take you back to where you came from must die.

When you are born again, any inherent weakness must be discarded. You can never become so strong that you will be able to live with those temptations again. Once you know your weak spot, run away from it.

Another lesson to learn from this story is that it was the sword of Goliath that David used to cut off his head. The solution to your problem is contained within the problem. That which will solve the problem is attached to the problem. The Bible is full of examples of this. When the enemies of Daniel wanted to destroy him, they threw him into the lions' den. He came out alive and the very people who threw him into the lions' den, were destroyed by God. What started as a problem for Daniel ended with the total eradication of his enemies.

There is also the example of Mordecai. The gallows that his enemy erected for him was used to hang the enemy. In 2 Chronicles 20:1-25, the kings that gathered against Jehoshaphat ended up destroying themselves. God has promised that enemies that come against us shall be smitten before us.

When the children of Israel saw that Goliath was fallen, they shouted. Shouting is part of our worship. Those that shout will be those who end up on the winning side. Do not allow the devil to silence you. When it is time to praise God, do not do so quietly. Do it as loudly as you can because it will show the Almighty God that you believe that you will overcome. He commands us to shout in Psalm 47:1:

"O clap your hands, all ye people; shout unto God with the voice of triumph."

He wants all His children to rejoice before Him by clapping and shouting in triumph. Can you shout when you are facing a problem? You should, because it tells Almighty God that you trust Him to provide a way out.

Chapter 21

---◆◆◆---

YOU CAN MAKE A COVENANT WITH GOD

1 Samuel 18:1-3:

"And it came to pass, when he had made an end of speaking unto Saul, that the soul of Jonathan was knit with the soul of David, and Jonathan loved him as his own soul. And Saul took him that day, and would let him go no more home to his father's house. Then Jonathan and David made a covenant, because he loved him as his own soul."

David had just defeated Goliath and had come before Saul. He introduced himself to Saul and was invited to stay. The first son of King Saul, Jonathan, was standing by and he began to demonstrate a very strange kind of love for David. They entered into a covenant.

DAVID AND JONATHAN MADE A COVENANT: YOU CAN MAKE A COVENANT WITH GOD

A covenant is a very powerful and irrevocable agreement between two parties. In Biblical times it used to be sealed with blood. Those who join secret societies still enter into covenants through blood. The first covenant between God and

Man that we want to refer to is the one between God and Abraham. There had been covenants before this, however. For example, God made a covenant with Noah where God said the sign of the rainbow would show that He would never flood the earth with water again.

The covenant between God and Abraham is described in Genesis 12, 15 and 17: In Jeremiah 17:9, the Bible tells us that the heart of Man is deceitful above all things and desperately wicked. Jesus Christ said in Matthew 15:17-20 that out of the heart proceeds all sorts of evil thoughts. When we talk about circumcision of the heart, just like the circumcision of the flesh, it should result in a change. Circumcision brings something new out of something bad. When God is talking about circumcision of the heart, He is talking of a brand new heart.

In 2 Corinthians 5:17, the Bible talks about becoming a new creature:

"There if any man be in Christ, he is a new creature: old things are passed away: behold, all things are become new."

You cannot become a new person unless you have a new heart. Becoming a child of God means asking for a new heart. The reason why many of us have found the Christian life very difficult is because we still retain the old heart. Until God takes away the old heart and gives you a new one, you cannot live the Christian life as you should.

Fortunately, God promised in Ezekiel 36:24-26 to give us a new heart if we ask for it:

"For I will take you from among the heathen, and gather you out of all countries, and will bring you into your own land. Then will I sprinkle clean water upon you, and ye shall be clean: from all your filthiness, and from all your idols, will I cleanse you. A new heart also will I give you, and a new spirit will I put within you: and I will take away the stony heart out of your flesh, and I will give you an heart of flesh."

Ask God for a new heart today. As long as you stay within the covenant, you will always be victorious. If you are outside the covenant, no matter how strong you are, you will keep on failing. This was why David called Goliath an uncircumcised Philistine. David knew that he would be victorious because he was under the covenant.

Chapter 22

SHOW OF LOVE

1 SAMUEL 18:4:

"And Jonathan stripped himself of the robe that was upon him, and gave it to David, and his garments, even to his sword, and to his bow, and to his girdle."

We have just been considering how Jonathan and David made a covenant. After this, Jonathan decided to give David certain objects. He gave him the robe that we was wearing, his garments, his sword, his bow and his girdle. All these things that Jonathan gave to David were very significant. A robe is something you wear to look beautiful. The other garments are worn so that you will not get cold. The sword is used for fighting. The bow is also used for fighting and hunting. In those days, the girdle was supposed to be where you kept your treasure, so that you tied it round yourself for safety.

Jonathan handed over all these things to David. We thank God for this because he was giving us an example of what Jesus Christ gave to the Church. He gave us His robe, other garments, everything else we need, whether it be sword, bow or girdle. In Isaiah 61:10 the Bible says:

"I will greatly rejoice in the LORD, my soul shall be joyful in my God; for he hath clothed me with the garments of salvation, he hath covered me with the robe of righteousness, as a bridegroom decketh himself with ornaments, and as a bride adorneth herself with her jewels."

Also, Psalm 132:16:

"I will also clothe her priests with salvation: and her saints shall shout aloud for joy."

The first thing God does when you come to Him is to clothe you with salvation. Even before God drove out Adam and Eve from the Garden of Eden, He clothed their nakedness. From that time till now, no matter how terrible your former life, if you turn to Almighty God, He will clothe you with salvation. He is ready to cover your shame. In Isaiah 61:3 when the Lord was talking about what He had come to the world to do, He said He has come to appoint unto them that mourn in Zion, to give unto them beauty for ashes. Also, He came to give them the oil of joy for mourning and the garment of praise for the spirit of heaviness. Therefore, God gives to us the robe of righteousness, the garment of salvation and the garment of praise.

Furthermore, He gives us all the equipment that we need to defend ourselves against the enemy. Jonathan gave to David his sword and his bow, although there were other items used in combat that were not included. There was no spear, no shield and no helmet. When God wants to give you something to defend yourself He gives you everything listed in Ephesians 6:10-17:

"Finally, my brethren, be strong in the Lord, and in the power of his might. Put on the whole armour of God, that ye may be able to stand against the wiles of the devil. For we wrestle not against flesh and blood, but against principalities, against powers, against the rulers of the darkness of this world, against spiritual wickedness in high places. Wherefore take unto you the whole armour of God, that ye may be able to withstand in the evil day, and having done all, to stand. Stand therefore, having your loins girt about with truth, and having on the breastplate of righteousness; And your feet shod with the preparation of the gospel of peace; Above all, taking the shield of faith, wherewith ye shall be able to quench all the fiery darts of the

wicked. And take the helmet of salvation, and the sword of the Spirit, which is the word of God."

God has given us all His weapons and armour. We have a girdle of truth, a breastplate of righteousness and our feet shod with the preparation of the gospel of peace. We also have the shield of faith, the helmet of salvation and the sword of the Spirit, which is the word of God. This sword is exceptionally sharp according to Hebrews 4:12:

"For the word of God is quick, and powerful, and sharper than any two-edged sword, piercing even to the dividing asunder of soul and spirit, and of the joints and marrow, and is a discerner of the thoughts and intents of the heart."

God has also given us all we need to neutralise any arrow of the enemy. Isaiah 54:17 says:

"No weapon that is formed against thee shall prosper; and every tongue that shall rise against thee in judgement thou shalt condemn. This is the heritage of the servants of the LORD, and their righteousness is of me, saith the LORD."

Also in Zechariah 2:5, the Bible says:

"For I, saith the LORD, will be unto her a wall of fire round about, and will be the glory in the midst of her."

So while Jonathan gave some beautiful things to David, Jesus Christ gave us something much more precious. There is something Jonathan did not give David that he could easily have given. These were the shoes on his feet. Look at Ruth 4:7:

"Now this was the manner in former time in Israel concerning redeeming and concerning changing, for to confirm all things; a man plucked off his shoe, and gave it to his neighbour: and this was a testimony in Israel."

To confirm all things, a man was expected to remove one shoe and give to his neighbour as a testimony in Israel. It was used as a testimony in any transaction.

Jonathan did not give David his shoes. This was another way of saying he could go back on his words and retrieve all the things he gave David.

Also, in these times in Israel, only sons in the family wore shoes. Servants were not allowed to wear shoes. In Luke 15:22 when the prodigal son returned home, his father asked his servants to dress him up and put shoes on his feet. It was another way of saying he had accepted him back as his son. Jonathan was saying here that even though they were friends, there was a limit to their friendship. John 8:35 sets out the distinction between sons and servants:

> *"And the servant abideth not in the house for ever: but the Son abideth ever."*

The son abides in the house while the servant will come and go. In 1 Samuel 20:41-42 after the discussion between Jonathan and David, Jonathan went back to the palace while David stayed in the countryside.

We thank God that Jesus Christ has come to make us sons forever. Because we are children of God, we have tremendous privileges. We can enter the throne room of God without invitation. You do not need an appointment. No angel can stop you. The greatest of the angels according to the word of God, is only a servant. Because God has made us children, according to Romans 8:15-17, everything that is available to Jesus Christ is available to us. This is one of the greatest blessings of being a child of God.

Jesus Christ will love us to the end (John 13:1). In John 15:14-15, Jesus calls us friends and no more servants. It is not a question of Him staying in the palace while we stay in the servants' quarters. Any separation between Him and us is only temporary. He said He was going to prepare a place for us so that where He is we will be also. Not only does He want us to live in the same place, according to Revelation 3:21, He wants us to sit with Him on His throne. He does not want there to be any separation between us at all.

Some people may ask how the throne can contain all of us? I do not know how big the throne is, but regardless of its size, I know that there is room for me there. My concern is not about those who will sit on the floor but where I will sit. I will be sitting near my Lord. Revelation 3:21 says:

"To him that overcometh will I grant to sit with me in my throne, even as I also overcame, and am set down with my Father in his throne."

I want to sit with Him on His throne. I want to be there, sitting down judging the nations of the world. How will I overcome? Romans 8:37 gives the answer:

"Nay, in all these things we are more than conquerors through him that loved us."

I will overcome through Him that loves me. From the passage above, I have deduced that the only thing God wants from me is love. Love is a two-way thing. If I can love Him the way He loves me, I will not sin, if I can love Him the way He loves me, I will need nobody to preach to me about serving Him. I will give anything I have to Him joyfully. Lord, help me to love you the way you love me.

Chapter 23

———◆◆◆———

DARKNESS AND LIGHT

1 Samuel 18:10-11:

> *"And it came to pass on the morrow, that the evil spirit from God came upon Saul, and he prophesied in the midst of the house: and David played with his hand, as at other times: and there was a javelin in Saul's hand. And Saul cast the javelin; for he said, I will smite David even to the wall with it. And David avoided out of his presence twice."*

The passage above is extremely interesting. There were two people in the house; King Saul from whom God had departed but who was still sitting on the throne and David whom God had anointed to succeed Saul who enjoyed God's presence. One was full of evil while the other was playing the harp. One was praising God; the other was seeking to use a weapon, to kill.

Two interesting things happened here. The one that was filled with the evil spirit began to prophesy while the one who was full of the Holy Spirit was praising God. King Saul then suddenly decided that he who was praising God must be killed. He threw his javelin with the intent of pinning him to the wall. The javelin missed David, King Saul missed twice, and David continued praising

God. The devil will keep on missing his target, no matter how many times he fires his arrow at you. We have two beautiful lessons to point out here. One is that even the devil can prophesy. The second is that darkness will always want to destroy light.

THREE SOURCES OF PROPHECY

There are three types of prophecy. The first type is that which is given by the Holy Spirit,. God the Holy Spirit can give you the ability to prophesy. In Acts 2:16-17, the Bible tells us that God had prophesied through Joel that in the last days, He will pour out His Spirit upon all flesh and our sons and daughters will prophesy. In other words, the gift of prophecy is available to young people. As for old men and women, He said they would dream dreams.

However, someone who says, 'Thus says the Lord', is not necessarily a prophet. A prophet is much more than this. A prophet should be able to teach, to pastor and be able to do the work of an evangelist. Prophecy comes from the Holy Spirit and it is always totally accurate. Even though it may appear difficult to believe, at the end of the day, it will come to pass.

The second type or source of prophecy is that which comes through the human spirit. According to 1 Thessalonians 5:23, man is a trinity. He is spirit. He has a soul and he lives inside the body. The real man is a spirit with a soul. These two dwell in the body. From time to time you find people who prophesy through their own spirit concerning something they want to happen or something they know that the people want to hear. Such instances include when a prophet sees a beautiful lady in the church and says the Lord has indicated she is his wife, or when the prophet prophesies that his sister will marry a rich man in the church. In Jeremiah 23:26-32, the word of God says that those who prophesy from their own heart will lead the people astray, in Jeremiah 14:15, God says He will destroy such prophets. It can be very dangerous if God is against you.

The third source of prophecy comes from demons. There is a very clear illustration of this in 1 Kings 22:1-23. God wanted to destroy King Ahab but He did not want him to die at home but on the battlefield. God called all His angels and the hosts of Heaven together to advise Him on what to do. One spirit then advised that he should be allowed to enter into the mouth of the prophets of Ahab and become a lying spirit. The advisers of Ahab said he should go to war and that he would win. Micaiah told him the truth – that he would not win. Of course, Ahab did not believe him. God is a merciful God and He is warning those who are in sin to cease. It will not be well with those who are living in sin, but it shall be well with the righteous.

1 John 4:1-3 admonishes us to try every spirit because not every spirit is from God. Acts 16:16 talks about the spirit of divination. This is the kind of spirit used by herbalists.

DARKNESS ALWAYS WANTS TO DESTROY LIGHT

Let us look at why Saul threw his javelin. What had David done to warrant the attack? Nothing, the devil does not wait for you to do anything wrong before he tries to attack you. It is inevitable that darkness will try to attack light. It is inevitable that witches and wizards will try to attack you. They will always seek to destroy. 1 Peter 5:8 says:

"Be sober, be vigilant; because your adversary the devil, as a roaring lion, walketh about, seeking whom he may devour:"

John 8:44 says:

"Ye are of your father the devil, and the lusts of your father ye will do. He was a murderer from the beginning, and abode not in the truth, because there is no truth in him. When he speaketh a lie, he speaketh of his own: for he is a liar, and the father of it."

John 10:10 adds:

"The thief cometh not, but for to steal, and to kill, and to destroy: I am come that they might have life, and that they might have it more abundantly."

You must not befriend anyone who is not on the Lord's side, although you should seek to win them for the Lord. The beauty of the story is that although Saul threw the javelin twice he missed twice. In other words, no matter how hard the enemy may try, as long as you belong to Almighty God, he will protect you from evil. Proverbs 21:31 says safety is of the Lord. David was praising the

Lord. God always protects those who know how to praise Him. In 2 Corinthians 1:8-10, Paul said:

"For we would not, brethren, have you ignorant of our trouble which came to us in Asia, that we were pressed out of measure, above strength, insomuch that we despaired even of life: But we had the sentence of death in ourselves, that we should not trust in ourselves, but in God which raiseth the dead: Who delivered us from so great a death, and doth deliver: in whom we trust that he will yet deliver us;"

God has delivered us in the past. He is delivering us now. He will deliver us in the future. If you are a true child of God, you do not have to worry about the attacks of the enemy. The One who has kept you alive to this day will continue to deliver you. Isaiah 54:17 says:

"No weapon that is formed against thee shall prosper; and every tongue that shall rise against thee in judgement thou shalt condemn. This is the heritage of the servants of the LORD, and their righteousness is of me, saith the LORD."

However, the above promise is subject to one condition, as in Psalm 91:1-8:

"He that dwelleth in the secret place of the most High shall abide under the shadow of the Almighty. I will say of the Lord, He is my refuge and my fortress: my God; in him will I trust. Surely he shall deliver thee from the snare of the fowler, and from the noisome pestilence. He shall cover thee with his feathers, and under his wings shalt thou trust: his truth shall be thy shield and buckler. Thou shalt not be afraid for the terror by night; nor for the arrow that flieth by day; Nor for the pestilence that walketh in darkness; nor for the destruction that wasteth at noonday. A thousand shall fall at thy side, and ten thousand at thy right hand; but it shall not come nigh thee. Only with thine eyes shalt thou behold and see the reward of the wicked."

If you dwell with the Almighty, He will deliver you. One of the reasons why holiness is a must for Christians is that darkness always faces light. Darkness never turns its back to light. Darkness is always watching for the moment when light becomes dim, then it pounces. Those who are in Christ must make sure that they do not leave Him. I am already in Him and I am going to stay in Him.

The enemy neither slumbers nor sleeps. You must to be holy all the time. You must pray all the time.

Chapter 24

FEAR AND THE BACKSLIDER

1 Samuel 18:12-16:

> *"And Saul was afraid of David, because the LORD was with him, and was departed from Saul. Therefore Saul removed him from him, and made him his captain over a thousand; and he went out and came in before the people. And David behaved himself wisely in all his ways; and the LORD was with him. Wherefore when Saul saw that he behaved himself very wisely, he was afraid of him. But all Israel and Judah loved David, because he went out and came in before them."*

THE PUNISHMENT FOR BACKSLIDING IS THAT A PERSON BECOMES FEARFUL

King Saul was afraid of David. Her had a good reason to be afraid, God was with David but had departed from Saul. Also, David was behaving himself wisely. The first punishment, indeed one of the worst punishments a backslider suffers – is that he becomes fearful. 1 John 4:18 says:

> *"There is no fear in love; but perfect love casteth out fear: because fear*

hath torment He that feareth is not made perfect in love."

Nothing torments a man like fear. When a man who used to be a friend of God becomes separated from God, fear will fill him. In Genesis 3:8-10, the Bible tells us that after Adam and Eve had eaten the forbidden fruit, their eyes were opened and they saw they were naked, suddenly they heard the voice of God and went to hide themselves.

Hitherto, when God drew near they had always rushed to meet Him. However, after they had sinned, they heard God's voice and became afraid. When a man backslides, he begins to fear all kinds of things because he no longer fears God. If you fear God, you will not sin. If you fear God, you will aim to avoid doing anything that will annoy Him. Psalm 53:4-5 says:

> *"Have the workers of iniquity no knowledge? who eat up my people as they eat bread: they have no called upon God. There were they in great fear, where no fear was: for God hath scattered the bones of him that encampeth against thee: thou has put them to shame, because God hath despised them."*

Whenever you find yourself being tormented by fear, check your walk with God; it may mean that you are far from Him. It may mean that the intimacy between you and God has been broken. There is a difference between fearing man and fearing God. The fear of God is pure. It is something you are thankful for. Psalm 19:9 says:

> *"The fear of the LORD is clean, enduring forever: the judgements of the LORD are true and righteous altogether."*

The kind of fear that you have for your father which prevents you disobeying him, is also a healthy fear. It is about discipline and reverence. As long as you have this kind of fear for God, you can enjoy His love, and His protection. If you fear God and do His will, you will have nothing to fear. David said in Psalm 27:1-3:

> *"The Lord is my light and my salvation; whom shall I fear? The Lord is the strength of my life; of whom shall I be afraid? When the wicked, even mine enemies and my foes, came upon me to eat up my flesh, they stumbled*

and fell. Though an host should encamp against me, my heart shall not fear: though war should rise against me, in this will I be confident."

"In God I will praise his word, in God I have put my trust; I will not fear what flesh can do unto me." Psalm 56:4

If you fear God, you can be confident that no man can harm you, for God will be on your side. The Bible makes it clear that as long as you are walking with God you have no need to fear.

The fear of God is the beginning of wisdom. It is the fear of the Lord that will cause you to depart from iniquity. It is the fear of the Lord that will prevent you from doing anything that will cause God to turn His face away from you. Make sure that you seek wisdom. Solomon said that of all the things one should seek, wisdom is among the most precious. In modern day language, we would say whatever you are seeking, make sure you find Christ.

1 Corinthians 1:24 says Christ is the wisdom of God:

"But unto them which are called, both Jews and Greeks, Christ the power of God, and the wisdom of God."

In other words, we could say, be willing to lose anything as long as you do not lose Christ. Do not let anything take your salvation away from you. Hold on to Him. He can take you from the dunghill and make you a prince. If you lose Christ, you have lost everything. I pray that you will never lose Christ.

There is another definition of wisdom: the correct application of knowledge. If you see a road sign that says 'Narrow Bridge Ahead' and you do not slow down and have an accident, you are a fool. You did not use the information supplied by the sign wisely. To act wisely means using the knowledge that you have.

HOW DO I ACT WISELY?

First, we must study the Bible to learn what God has said. Second, apply that knowledge you have acquired rightly. For example, I have learnt from the Bible about the law of harvest and I have been putting it into use, I have learnt that I will get a hundredfold return on whatever I give. A man who wins souls conscientiously is merely acting wisely on the knowledge they have gained from John 15:16:

> *"Ye have not chosen me, but I have chosen you, and ordained you, that ye should go and bring forth fruit, and that your fruit should remain: that whatsoever ye shall ask of the Father in my name, he may give it you."*

The secret of answered prayers can be found when you win souls and follow them up. I pay my tithes because I have learnt that if I pay my tithe, devourers will be rebuked for my sake. The windows of heaven must open for me because I am acting wisely. I want the kind of blessing that there will not be room enough to contain.

The Bible says God inhabits the praises of His people. This means that if you praise Him, He will draw near to you. Anytime you feel as if God is far away, you should apply this piece of knowledge and start praising Him.

When Jesus Christ says unless you are born again you cannot see the Kingdom of God, if you are wise, you will give your life to Christ. Act wisely now and He will receive you. His blood will cleanse you from all your sins and you will find your name is written in the Book of Life.

Chapter 25

THE SNARE OF THE FOWLER

1 Samuel 18:17-27:

"And Saul said to David, Behold my elder daughter Merab, her will I give thee to wife: only be thou valiant for me, and fight the Lord's battles. For Saul said, Let not mine hand be upon him, but let the hand of the Philistines be upon him. And David said unto Saul, Who am I? And what is my life, or my father's family in Israel, that I should be son in law to the King? But it came to pass at the time when Merab Saul's daughter should have been given to David, that she was given unto Adriel the Meholathite to wife. And Michal Saul's daughter loved David: and they told Saul, and the thing pleased him. And Saul said, I will give him her, that she may be a snare to him and that the hand of the Philistines may be against him. Wherefore Saul said to David, Thou shalt this day be my son in law in the one of the twain. And Saul commanded his servants, saying, Commune with David secretly, and say, Behold, the king hath delight in thee, and all his servants love thee: now therefore be the king's son in law. And Saul's servants spake those words in the ears of David. And David said, Seemeth it to you a light thing to be a king's son in law, seeing that I am a poor man, and lightly

esteemed? And the servants of Saul told him, saying, On this manner spake David. And Saul said, Thus shall ye say to David, The king desireth not any dowry, but an hundred foreskins of the Philistines, to be avenged of the king's enemies. But Saul thought to make David fall by the hand of the Philistines. And when his servants told David these words, it pleased David well to be the king's son in law: and the days were not expired. Wherefore David arose and went, he and his men, and slew of the Philistines two hundred men; and David brought their foreskins, and they gave them in full tale to the king, that he might be the king's son in law. And Saul gave him Michal his daughter to wife."

BEWARE OF THE SNARE OF THE FOWLER

Saul told David that he wanted him to be his son in law. He decided that as he could not kill David himself the Philistines would kill him instead. David refused the offer. Saul found out that his younger daughter was in fact in love with David, He then tried to give this daughter as a snare to David.

Because Saul had become a backslider, he became an agent of the devil. You cannot trust anyone or somebody who is not living a holy life. According to John 8:44, the devil is a liar and the father of lies. This means that anybody who is a liar is a child of the devil. The devil can never tell the truth. Backsliders never tell the truth. This is why God says there will be no room for liars in heaven. If you are still lying, whether you regard your life as yellow, white or black lies, you know who your father is. If you will enjoy lying, you must seek salvation because once you become a true child of God, lying will lose its appeal for you.

Any time the devil offers you something, you can be sure that there is a trap somewhere. Whenever the devil is asking you to take something that you know is contrary to the will of God, you can be sure that there is a price to pay. Beware of the snare of the fowler. There is somebody who is hunting for your soul.

In Genesis 3:1-10, the devil lured Adam and Eve into eating the forbidden fruit. The devil told them that God did not want them to eat the fruit to prevent them becoming like Him. Did they become like God when they ate the fruit?

Certainly not. They found out that they were naked and that the glory of God had departed from them. In 2 Corinthians 12:9, God told Paul that His grace was sufficient for him. If you are finding things difficult now, but keep holding on to God, you will surely have the last laugh. If you are on the side of the Lord and you refuse to bend, His grace will be sufficient for you.

Two brothers were arrested in a communist country because they were Christians. They were told if they would deny Jesus Christ they would go free, but otherwise they would be burnt alive. They decided not to deny Jesus Christ. The two of them agreed that when the fire was burning, if His grace was sufficient, they should raise a finger. If His grace was not sufficient, they should wave their hands. As the fire began to burn, the older brother looked at the younger one and raised his finger, to show him that the grace of God was sufficient for him. The younger brother looked back and instead of raising a finger, he raised two fingers. His grace is more than sufficient. If you are going through fire now, I can assure you that His grace is more than sufficient.

Chapter 26

---◆---

A GREATER FRIEND THAN JONATHAN

1 Samuel 19:1-7:

"And Saul spake to Jonathan his son, and to all his servants, that they should kill David. But Jonathan Saul's son delighted much in David: and Jonathan told David, saying, Saul my father seeketh to kill thee: now therefore, I pray thee, take heed to thyself until the morning, and abide in a secret place, and hide thyself: and I will go out and stand beside my father in the field where thou art, and I will commune with my father of thee; and what I see, that I will tell thee. And Jonathan spake good of David unto Saul his father, and said unto him Let not the king sin against his servant, against David; because he hath not sinned against thee, and because his works have been to thee-ward very good: for he did put his life in his hand, and slew the Philistine, and the Lord wrought a great salvation for all Israel: thou sawest it, and didst rejoice: wherefore then wilt thou sin against innocent blood, to slay David without a cause? And Saul hearkened unto the voice of Jonathan: and Saul sware, As the Lord liveth, he shall not be slain. And Jonathan called David, and Jonathan shewed him all those things. And Jonathan brought David to Saul, and he was in his presence, as in times past."

WE HAVE A GREATER FRIEND THAN JONATHAN

After Saul failed to trap David through his daughter, he now openly ordered Jonathan and his servants to kill David. Jonathan quickly went to advise David to go into hiding. He said he would talk to his father and if all was well, he David could return to Saul's service, Jonathan showed himself a good friend to David, but thank God, we have a better friend than Jonathan. This Friend is Jesus Christ. Jonathan was able to pacify his father for a brief moment so that David would not die. The Almighty God has provided us with a Friend so that we will not die, for He died in our place. John 14:6 says:

> *"Jesus saith unto him, I am the way, the truth, and the life: no man cometh unto the Father, but by me."*

Jonathan was able to reconcile David back to his father for a short while. When Jesus reconciles you to Almighty God, it is permanent. Ephesians 2:18-19 says:

> *"For through him we both have access by one Spirit unto the Father. Now therefore ye are no more strangers and foreigners, but fellow citizens with the saints, and of the household of God:"*

Although Jonathan was able to reconcile David to his father, he was still a stranger in the king's house. Through Jesus Christ we are reconciled to God permanently, and will no longer be strangers. We will no longer be foreigners. We will become members of the household of God, Ephesians 2:11 and 14 says:

> *"Wherefore remember, that ye being in time past Gentiles in the flesh, who are called Uncircumcision by that which is called the Circumcision in the flesh made by hands."*

> *"For he is our peace, who hath made both one, and hath broken down the middle wall of partition between us."*

There was a time when a gentile woman came to Jesus Christ and said that she needed help. Jesus told her that He was not sent but to the lost sheep of the house of Israel. In another place the Bible says salvation is of the Jews. Gentiles and foreigners were without hope but Jesus Christ has brought us near. The word of God says for as many as received Him, to them gave He the power to become the sons of God. Those who are born again are now the true Israelites.

In John 14:1-3, Jesus Christ tells us that there are many mansions is His Father's house and He has gone to prepare a place for us. When He finishes the preparation, he will come back to take us home so that where He is we will be also, not for a short time but forever. Jonathan was a very good advocate. We have a greater advocate, according to 1 John 2:1-2, who is pleading our cause every day, free of charge:

"My little children, these things write I unto you, that ye sin not. And if any man sin, we have an advocate with the Father, Jesus Christ the righteous: And he is the propitiation for our sins: and not for our's only, but also for the sins of the whole world."

When you confess your sin and repent, He will plead your case with the Father. This is why we should praise the Lord Jesus Christ every day.

UNTIL YOU MORTIFY YOUR FLESH YOU ARE A SPLIT PERSONALITY

Jonathan spoke with his father and suddenly Saul started behaving like a normal human being. He said David was an honourable man and should not be killed. As we will discover, however, later, the evil in him resurfaced again later, and he planned once more to kill David. We therefore find in King Saul two personalities. A part of him wanted to do good while the other part wanted to do evil. This is a very graphic illustration of the struggles of the flesh. Unless you do something about it, you will find your life being controlled by two personalities. One is called the spirit while the other is called the flesh. There is always a constant battle between the spirit and the flesh. As a Christian, for example, you know that you must do good but from time to time somebody causes you to sin. In my first two years as a Christian, I had many such battles. I thank God that now I have got my victory. In Galatians 5:16-17, the Bible says:

"This I say then, Walk in the Spirit and ye shall not fulfil the lust of the flesh. For the flesh lusteth against the Spirit, and the Spirit against the flesh: and

these are contrary the one to the other: so that ye cannot do the things that ye would."

The spirit and the flesh are always in constant battle. If you decide tonight that you are going to start a fast tomorrow at 6 a.m., it is hunger that will wake you up. If you do not want to fast, you may not even remember to eat until 3 p.m. This is the resistance of the flesh at work. These two personalities are listed in Galatians 5:19-23.

> *"Now the works of the flesh are manifest, which are these; Adultery, fornication, uncleanness, lasciviousness, idolatry, witchcraft, hatred, variance, emulations, wrath, strife, seditions, heresies, envyings, murders, drunkenness, revellings, and such like: of the which I tell you before, as I have also told you in time past, that they which do such things shall not inherit the kingdom of God. But the fruit of the Spirit is love, joy, peace, longsuffering, gentleness, goodness, faith, meekness, temperance: against such there is no law."*

Unless God gives you victory, it will be difficult to escape the works of the flesh. The path you decide to take will determine whether you become a friend of God or remain His enemy. If you surrender to the flesh, you will become God's enemy and no enemy of God will enter His Kingdom. The Bible tells us repeatedly what we must do to be victorious over the flesh. Ephesians 4:17-25 talks of putting on the new man:

> *"This I say therefore, and testify in the Lord, that ye henceforth walk not as other Gentiles walk, in the vanity of their mind, Having the understanding darkened, being alienated from the life of God through the ignorance that is in them, because of the blindness of their heart: Who being past feeling have given themselves over unto lasciviousness, to work all uncleanness with greediness. But yet have not so learned Christ; If so be that ye have heard him, and have been taught by him, as the truth is in Jesus: That ye put off concerning the former conversation the old man, which is corrupt according to the deceitful lusts; And be renewed in the spirit of your mind; And that ye put on the new man, which after God is created in righteousness and true holiness. Wherefore putting away lying, speak every man truth with his neighbour: for we are members one of another."*

Ephesians 4:28-31 continues:

"Let him that stole steal no more: but rather let him labour, working with his hands the thing which is good, that he may have to give to him that needeth. Let no corrupt communication proceed out of your mouth, but that which is good to the use of edifying, that it may minister grace unto the hearers. And grieve not the holy Spirit of God, whereby ye are sealed unto the day of redemption. Let all bitterness, and wrath, and anger, and clamour, and evil speaking, be put away from you, with all malice:"

Romans 8:12-13 says:

"Therefore, brethren, we are debtors, not to the flesh, to live after the flesh. For if ye live after the flesh, ye shall die: but if ye through the Spirit do mortify the deeds of the body, ye shall live."

To mortify the flesh means to put to death, that part of the body that is about to cause you trouble. A far better solution is in Galations 5:24:

"And they that are Christ's have crucified the flesh with the affections and lusts."

The company you keep can influence your mind. The type of sermons you hear can influence your mind. If you hear a message on faith, your faith will grow. If you hear a message on holiness, you will want to live a holy life. If you hear a message on doubt, you will start to doubt. My belief in divine healing grew because I heard a testimony about healing. Years later when I heard a preacher on television say that you cannot rely on God hundred percent for divine healing, I switched off my television set. I did not want him to kill my faith.

In the past I used to be very angry but now God has solved my problem. I have since discovered that any man who gets angry is the type of person who considers himself important. This is a work of the flesh. When the flesh is dead, you are nobody. You are nothing. I know that without Jesus Christ I am nothing so when anybody insults me, I keep quiet. When a man is dead, there is nothing you can do to him to make him angry. If you want to be victorious over anger, wrath and over all things of the flesh, you must be dead to the flesh.

If you are truly determined, you can obtain total freedom from the flesh, but if you are not yet a Christian, you are at present an enemy of God. In fact, in your own case, it is only the flesh that is at work. You can go to the Lord and ask Him to save your soul, and then if you ask Him to do so He will crucify your flesh too.

Chapter 27

THE ENEMY IS DECEITFUL

1 Samuel 19:8-17:

"And there was war again: and David went out, and fought with the Philistines, and slew them with a great slaughter; and they fled from him. And the evil spirit from the LORD was upon Saul, as he sat is his house with his javelin in his hand: and David played with his hand. And Saul sought to smite David even to the wall with the javelin; but he slipped away out of Saul's presence, and he smote the javelin into the wall: and David fled, and escaped that night. Saul also sent messengers unto David's house, to watch him, and to slay him in the morning: and Michal David's wife told him, saying, If thou save not thy life to night, tomorrow thou shalt be slain. So Michal let David down through a window: and he went, and fled, and escaped. And Michal took an image, and laid it in the bed, and put a pillow of goats' hair for his bolster, and covered it with a cloth. And when Saul sent messengers to take David, she said, He is sick. And Saul sent the messengers again to see David, saying. Bring him up to me in the bed, that I may slay him. And when the messengers were come in, behold, there was an image in the bed, with a pillow of goats' hair for his bolster. And Saul said unto Michal, Why hast thou

deceived me so, and sent away mine enemy, that he is escaped? And Michal answered Saul, He said unto me, Let me go; why should I kill thee?"

This is an extremely interesting section of the story of David. The Bible says there was war once again. The Philistines came back. They were determined to avenge their defeat. David went out again and slaughtered them and they fled from him. One would think this would please King Saul. Instead, he became more enraged. While David was playing on the harp, King Saul threw a javelin at him. David, being alert, was able to dodge it.

We have a lesson to learn here. Whenever your enemies say they have no more problem with you do not rely on the statement. You cannot rely on the promises of the enemy. The only promise you can rely on is that of the Almighty God. God has promised that you will be more than a conqueror.

David ran out of the palace. His wife, Saul's daughter, told him that her father was determined to kill him and that he should run away. David escaped with the help of his wife who let him down with a rope through the window. Before King Saul knew what was happening, David had gone far away. Before your enemies get to your doorstep, you will be gone, in Jesus' Name. Almighty God will always stand by you and give you victory.

Here, we want to concentrate on the duty of the wife to the husband. When God made woman, it was to be a helpmeet for the man. Any wife who is not helping her husband is failing in her purpose in life. Anyone who is failing in his or her purpose in life, is like a corpse walking about. It is the duty of every wife to support her husband.

In the Bible, you will find great women who did incredible things for their husbands. One example is Sarah. She is supposed to be the mother of all women of faith. In Genesis 12:10-20, the Bible tells us of a great sacrifice that Sarah made to protect Abraham. In Egypt, Sarah agreed to pretend to be Abraham's sister . At sixty-five, she was still beautiful and Abraham suspected Pharaoh might may want to harm him so as to marry Sarah. Pharaoh indeed took Sarah as his wife but spared Abraham. However, God intervened, and plagued the king's house. Pharaoh consulted his oracle and was told the problem. He asked Sarah to go back to her husband. He did not take back the gifts he had earlier given Abraham. He also decreed that nobody should harm them. Sarah had laid her life on the line to protect her husband.

In 1 Samuel 25:2-34, we meet another great woman, Abigail, who stood between her husband and death. God honoured her for this. Although her husband died because God had so determined, he made provision for her.

Matthew 19:5-6 says:

> *"And said, For this cause shall a man leave father and mother, and shall cleave to his wife: and they twain shall be one flesh? Wherefore they are no more twain, but one flesh. What therefore God hath joined together, let not man put asunder."*

When you marry, your loyalties change. In other words, if you have to choose between your husband and your father, your husband must come first.

Why must a wife support her husband so much? It is because the Bible says in Ephesians 5:23 that the husband is the head of the wife:

> *"For the husband is the head of the wife, even as Christ is the head of the church: and he is the saviour of the body."*

The wife can be viewed as the body of the husband. If the head dies, the whole body will be dead. From the moment something goes wrong with the head, the whole body will malfunction. When something goes wrong with the husband, the wife will be in trouble. Any wife that has any sense at all will therefore do everything possible to make sure that all is well with her husband.

In Ephesians 5:23 the Bible says Christ is the Head of the church. Christ is the husbands of the church, therefore we Christians have a great responsibility to our Lord. As a matter of fact, the Bible says in 1 Corinthians 6:15-20 that our own husband, Christ, lives in us and we are His temples, therefore we must keep the temples clean. This is why He said we must not commit adultery or fornication because our bodies are no longer ours; they belong to Christ.

Just as the wife is supposed to love her husband, the Bible says in Deuteronomy 6:5 that we are to love our Lord with all our heart, with all our mind and with all our strength:

"And thou shalt love the LORD thy God with all thine heart, and with all thy soul, and with all thy might."

We are to love Him above all else. In fact, according to Luke 14:26, Jesus Christ said when it comes to comparing the love for Him and the love for your parents, your love for Him must be so great that the love for your parents could be compared to hatred. He said if you are not willing to love Him that much, you cannot be His disciple. When Paul the apostle was told that he should avoid going to Jerusalem lest he would be bound, in Acts 21:13, he said he was not only ready to be imprisoned but also ready to die for Christ. I am ready to die for Christ. I am ready to give my life to defend the Name of my Husband.

In our relationship with Jesus Christ, everything we do or will ever do is because we are connected to Him. In John 15:5, Jesus Christ said that without Him we can do nothing. In Acts 17:28, we are told that in Him we live, move and have our being. In other words, without Christ, you cannot even move your hands or legs, or breathe. Everything we are is embedded in Him. Philippians 4:19 says God shall supply all our needs according to his riches in glory, through Christ Jesus.

CHOICES

Put yourself in the position of Michal. This woman had a big choice to make:- her father or her husband. This woman made the right choice. She chose her husband. Life is a continuous succession of choices. What you choose will determine what your future will be like. Some choices are simple while others are very complicated. Some choices affect your life forever. Once you choose your spouse for example, it is for life. Divorce is not recognised in Heaven. Only death can separate husband and wife.

When you have a choice to make, it is like you are at a crossroads. You have to decide whether to turn left or turn right. The moment you make your decision, things will begin to happen. By the time you decide to turn back, the person has chosen the other route is already far ahead of you. Choice is a serious matter.

In Deuteronomy 30:19-20, God said to the children of Israel, as He is saying to all of us today:

"I call heaven and earth to record this day against you, that I have set before you life and death, blessing and cursing: therefore choose life, that both thou and thy seed may live: That thou mayest love the LORD thy God, and that thou mayest obey his voice, and that thou mayest cleave unto him: for his is thy life, and the length of thy days: that thou mayest dwell in the land which the LORD sware unto thy fathers, to Abraham, to Isaac, and to Jacob, to give them."

God says you should choose life so that you and your children may live. In Hebrews 11:24-26, we are told that when Moses was growing in the palace of Pharaoh, he must have thought he was a prince. When he grew up he discovered that he was a Hebrew. He had to choose between continuing as a prince or becoming a slave. I would rather be a slave on the side of God than a prince on the side of Satan. Moses chose to be a slave and because of this choice, today, his name is recognised all over the world. His name is honoured in Christianity, in Islam and in Judaism. He became a deliverer. Initially, because of his choice, he was forced to become a fugitive for forty years, but after this, he became a terror to Pharaoh.

Esther was asked to choose between her people and remaining as queen. Esther chose to be on the side of the Lord. She did not perish. Her name is written in the Book of Life and we read about her today.

Shadrach, Meshach and Abednego had a terrible choice to make in Daniel 3. The king said if they did not bow before his golden image, they would burn. They could have chosen to bow down, as they were in another man's land. However, they said they would not bow down. They were thrown into the fiery furnace but Almighty God was there with them.

Daniel had a choice. In Daniel 6:6-10, a decree was enacted stating that if anybody prayed to any god or any man apart from the emperor during the following thirty days, they would be thrown into the lions' den. Daniel could have asked God to be excused praying for the thirty days. He could have decided to pray in secret. He knew they were forcing him to choose between his God and the government. He opened his windows wide and chose God. He was thrown into the lions' den but God was there with him too.

God never fails His own. The choice may be difficult, especially when God allows those who choose Him to suffer as a result. He does so in order that they would have a testimony. When Shadrach, Meshach and Abednego came out of the fiery furnace, Nebuchadnezzar said there was no one like their God. When Daniel came out of the lions' den his enemies perished in one day.

You have to choose. Many Christians today are so like the world that it is difficult to distinguish them. Nowadays, we hardly know who is a Christian and who is not. Sooner or later, the call will be heard, as it was by the children of Israel in Exodus 32:26: 'Who is on the Lord's side?' Moses had gone up to the presence of God to collect the Ten Commandments and before he returned, the children of Israel had called on Aaron to make a god for them, Aaron consented, and when Moses came down and saw this, he lifted up his voice and asked who was on the Lord's side. The children of Levi moved to his side and this removed the curse which had been put on them earlier.

When you choose to be on the Lord's side, you must be prepared to say what the Lord Jesus Christ said in Matthew 26:39:

> *"O my Father, if it be possible, let this cup pass from me: nevertheless not as I will, but as thou wilt."*

This is what it means to be on the Lord's side. You have to choose today which side you are going to be. How committed are you going to be to the Lord? I am on the Lord's side and I am going to remain on the Lord's side.

In 1979, I had to choose between attending a congress on December 24 and staying with my dying mother at home. I went to visit her and I told her that I had to attend the congress. She understood, thank God. That was a test. God wanted to see which option I would choose. My mother did not die then. She lived for another eleven years.

In 1981, one of my sons was brought home seriously ill. At this time, I had to go on a preaching engagement. I had to choose between being with my son and doing God's work. I committed him into the hands of God and left for my engagement. This was my son who married in 1995. Glory be to God.

Years ago, in a Communist country, if you said you were a Christian, they would kill you. A Christian lady was about to get married and she was told to deny Jesus and keep her freedom or accept Him and be arrested. It was her wedding day. She smiled and stretched out her hands for the handcuffs. She kissed the handcuffs and said, 'My Lord, I know you would not let any ordinary man marry me. How beautiful is this wedding ring!' They led her away to be killed.

Some time ago, in a Communist country, one day when some Christians were worshiping God secretly, some soldiers came in and asked them to choose between God and sudden death. They asked those who wanted to choose God to stay in the place and be killed while those who wanted to live should file out. Some people ran. The others said that if they wanted, they could shoot them. The soldiers then put down their guns, shut the door and joined in the worship. They said they were Christians too and that they had to use that method to make sure that no one reported them. Who is on the Lord's side? The choice is yours.

Chapter 28

THERE IS A TIME TO RUN

1 Samuel 19:18

"So David fled, and escaped, and came to Samuel to Ramah, and told him all that Saul had done to him. And he and Samuel went and dwelt in Naioth."

There are people who believe that you should never run once you become a child of God. There is no doubt that there are certain things that a child of God should not run away from. It is not appropriate for a child of God to run away from demons. We are to cast them out; even the The devil himself should be afraid of you. We are not to run from witches and wizards because even their boss, the devil, is under our feet.

However, there are certain things that we must run away from 2 Timothy 2:22 says:

"Flee also youthful lusts: but follow righteousness, faith, charity, peace, with them that call on the Lord out of a pure heart."

To flee means to run away in terror. We are to run away from youthful lusts.

They can kill faster than any poison. God expects you to run when somebody is trying to lure you into sin.

According to Proverbs 22:24-25, the Lord expects you also to flee from an angry man. If you keep the company of an angry man, you will learn his ways and he will become a snare for your soul.

In Proverbs 1:10-16, the Bible says if anyone is trying to entice you into committing a sin, you are to flee from them. It says that when sinners entice you do not consent; you are to flee. As a sister, if you go and greet a brother and he starts making advances at you, do not start arguing with him. It is not the time for Bible studies. You are to run. You can preach to him later, if you are in an environment where there is no danger. In 1 Corinthians 6:18, the Bible says:

"Flee fornication. Every sin that a man doeth is without the body; but he that committeth fornication sinneth against his own body."

You are to run from fornication. It is not something to treat lightly or frivolously. You should run from this danger that can kill you.

Ephesians 5:3-8 says:

"But fornication, and all uncleanness, or covetousness, let it not be once named among you, as becometh saints; Neither filthiness, nor foolish talking, nor jesting, which are not convenient: but rather giving of thanks. For this ye know, that no whoremonger, nor unclean person, nor covetous man, who is an idolater, hath any inheritance in the kingdom of Christ and of God. Let no man deceive you with vain words: for because of these things cometh the wrath of God upon the children of disobedience. Be not ye therefore partakers with them. For ye were sometimes darkness, but now are ye light in the Lord: walk as children of light;"

When you know that the wrath of God is about to fall on certain people, you should not stay near them. Stay clear of anybody that will bring you into conflict with God. Take advice only from somebody who is climbing and not from someone who is descending. James 4:6 says:

"But he giveth more grace. Wherefore he saith, God resisteth the proud, but giveth grace unto the humble."

Flee from pride. God resists the proud. You should run from anyone God resists. Romans 1:18 says:

> *"For the wrath of God is revealed from heaven against all ungodliness and unrighteousness of men, who hold the truth in unrighteousness"*

Do not become involved with anything that is contrary to the will of God. Run away from it. Joseph, in Genesis 39:7-12 ran away from committing fornication. Though his flight landed him in prison, he still ended up on the throne. Flee from anything that will cause you to annoy God. Every child of God must run from anything that will cause God to become angry.

WHEN YOU HAVE TO FLEE, RUN TO YOUR SOURCE

David fled to Samuel. This was a very wise decision. He knew that he was the source of his anointing. When there is trouble, go back to the source of your anointing. In the scriptures, we meet many people who came face to face with tremendous problems and when they had to run, they ran to their source.

In 2 Chronicles 20:1-3, we meet a king called Jehoshaphat. Three kings came up against him. Jehoshaphat sought his to God. At the end of the day, not only did God give him victory, but he ended up richer than before.

In Exodus 14:15, when the children of Israel had reached the Red Sea and the enemy was coming behind, the people cried unto Moses. Moses in turn ran to his source. He went back to God. God answered him and gave him the solution.

In Joshua 7:6-9, the Bible tells us that after the children of Israel were defeated by a small city called Ai, Joshua ran to God. God told him the solution. When you run back to your source, you will get an answer to your problem.

In 2 Kings 4:18-26, we read of the sadness of the Shunamite woman. Elisha prophesied that she would have a son and so she did. Then the child suddenly died. This woman took the child and laid him on the bed of the man of God and closed the door. She ran back to Elisha – her source of happiness. Elisha sent Gehazi raise her son, but he was unable to do so. It was Elisha who gave the son back to his mother alive. At the end of the day, her sorrow became double joy.

Judges 16:22 and 28, contains the final episode in the life of Samson. Samson had been disobedient. God had told him that no razor must touch his head, he must not drink wine and must not touch any corpse. He received great strength. One day after killing a lion, on his way back, he saw honey in the carcass of the lion and he ate it. Nothing happened to him so he continued in disobedience. He then visited a harlot. Still his strength remained intact so he carried on disobeying God. He eventually married Delilah, an enemy Philistine. He told her his secret and she cut off his hair. His strength left him, but God was merciful to him and his hair began to grow again. While his enemies were mocking his defeat, he cried once more unto God and God graciously strengthened him.

If you are a backslider, if you go back to your source, He will have mercy. The one who is your source is the Alpha and the Omega. He gave an invitation in John 7:37-38 that anyone that thirsts should come to Him. If you find yourself drying up and you have to flee, run back to your source. Go back and get fresh oil so that your fire can begin to burn again. Go and recharge your battery. Seek fresh fire from God. This is the only way to survive.

If you are not yet bornagain, come to the Source. Come to the Alpha and Omega. Come to the Word who was from the beginning. Come to the One who made you. Come to the One who can give you victory over your enemies.

Chapter 29

---◆---

THE ROCK OF AGES

1 Samuel 19:19-24:

"And it was told Saul, saying, Behold, David is at Naioth in Ramah. And Saul sent messengers to take David: and when they saw the company of the prophets prophesying, and Samuel standing as appointed over them, the Spirit of God was upon the messengers of Saul, and they also prophesied. And when it was told Saul, he sent other messengers, and; they prophesied likewise. And Saul sent messengers again the third time, and they prophesied also. Then went he also to Ramah, and came to a great well that is in Sechu: and he asked and said, Where are Samuel and David? And one said, Behold, they be at Naioth in Ramah. And he went thither to Naioth in Ramah: and the Spirit of God was upon him also, and he went on, and prophesied, until he came to Naioth in Ramah. And he stripped off his clothes also, and prophesied before Samuel in like manner, and lay down naked all that day and all that night. Wherefore they say, Is Saul also among the prophets?"

When Saul sent messengers to arrest David, the Holy Spirit arrested them instead. Soldiers suddenly became prophets. They began to prophesy. Saul sent another group when the first group did not come back. The same thing happened to them. Saul sent a third group and the same thing happened again. He then decided to go himself. Before he got there, the Spirit arrested him too. He forgot what he went to do. Any enemy coming to your house will forget what he is coming to do.

There is a difference between King Saul and the messengers he sent. The messengers were merely obeying orders while King Saul was the troublemaker. God arrested him and disgraced him. Picture the spectacle of a king removing all his clothes and lying down naked before his servant's for a whole day! May God disgrace your enemies.

God has several ways of dealing with the enemies of those who trust in Him. We will mention seven of these ways.

1 The first is for God to be a wall of fire round about His own, as in Zechariah 2:5:

> *"For I, saith the LORD, will be unto her a wall of fire round about, and will be the glory in the midst of her."*

In other words, ordinary eyes may not see this wall but if you truly belong to Jesus Christ, there is a wall of fire about you that no witch can pass through.

2 The second way is for God to neutralise the weapons of the enemy, in other words, if the enemies say they are going to use charms against you, God will cause the charms to be ineffective. Isaiah 54:17 confirms this:

> *"No weapon that is formed against thee shall prosper; and every tongue that shall rise against thee in judgment thou shalt condemn. This is the heritage of the servants of the LORD, and their righteousness is of me, saith the LORD."*

When Daniel was thrown into the lions' den, the Lord shut the mouths of the lions. When Shadrach, Meshach and Abednego were thrown into the fire, the power of fire was suddenly neutralised.

3 The third way in which God can defend you against your enemies is by paralysing them.

This is what David meant in Psalm 23:5:

"Thou prepares a table before me in the presence of mine enemies thou anointest my head with oil; my cup runneth over."

In other words, you are to sit down and enjoy yourself. The enemy will be watching but will not be able to do anything. He can paralyse them physically, as he did to Goliath. Goliath saw the stone coming towards his head but could not dodge it because he had been paralysed. God can also paralyse the enemy mentally and spiritually, as in the example above. The soldiers started prophesying instead of arresting David.

4   The fourth way is that God could decide to wipe out the enemy completely. God knows the various categories of our enemies. There are some enemies that should not be allowed to live. God knows that the best thing to do to these is to wipe them out because He knows those who will repent and those who will not repent. God destroyed Pharaoh and his soldiers at the Red Sea (Exodus 14:27-28). Daniel's enemies, who would never have left him in peace, al perished by God's provider in the lions' den. A similar fate befell those who ganged up against Moses in Numbers 16

5   The fifth way in which God can deal with your enemies is by uprooting them. A good example is found in Acts 13:6-12. Paul was preaching to a Governor but a sorcerer tried to defer him from responding. God did not want to kill the sorcerer so He merely made him blind for a while, so that Paul could win the soul of the Governor.

6   The sixth method God can use is to disgrace the enemy, as He did to King Saul, as mentioned above. In Acts 16:35-39, those who threw Paul and Silas into prison were disgraced after they had been set free.

7   The seventh way is by converting them. God can change your enemies to become your best friends. A very good example is Saul of Tarsus. He was a terrible man, raging against Christians and putting them into prison. God took hold of him and turned him into an apostle.

There is absolute security when you are hiding in the Rock of Ages. Psalm 91 states clearly that no evil will come near you at all once you have made the

Almighty God your refuge. He said you would be secure day and night. Many times, however, when we talk about enemies, we are referring to external enemies, but our number one enemy is inside us. It could be a desire to sin. It could be anger, impatience, or gluttony. You must deal with the enemy within before it disgraces you. If you do not destroy the enemy within you, it will end up destroying you.

Chapter 30

---◆◆◆---

ALWAYS AVOID ANGER

1 Samuel 20:27-34

In the early verses of 1 Samuel 20, the writer tells us how David came back to the palace and met Jonathan. He told Jonathan that Saul wanted to kill him but Jonathan was not convinced. They reached an agreement. David would hide in a bush while Jonathan would find out if King Saul wanted to kill David and then report back. If it was true that King Saul was after the life of David, Jonathan was to take a small boy, shoot an arrow beyond where he was and ask the boy to look beyond him. This was to be a sign that David must flee.

When it was time to eat in the palace, the absence of David was noticed and King Saul asked after him. Jonathan told his father that David asked for permission to go and offer a sacrifice in his home town and he had allowed him. What happened next is recorded in

1 Samuel 20:27-34:

> *"And it came to pass on the morrow, which was the second day of the month, that David's place was empty: and Saul said unto Jonathan his son, Wherefore cometh not the son of Jesse to meat, neither yesterday, nor*

146

today? And Jonathan answered Saul, David earnestly asked leave of me to go to Bethlehem: And he said, Let me go, I pray thee; for our family hath a sacrifice in the city; and my brother, he hath commanded me to be there: and now, if I have found favour in thine eyes, let me get away, I pray thee, and see my brethren. Therefore he cometh not unto the king's table. Then Saul's anger was kindled against Jonathan, and he said unto him, Thou son of the perverse rebellious woman, do not I know that thou hast chosen the son of Jesse to thine own confusion, and unto the confusion of thy mother's nakedness? For as long as the son of Jesse liveth upon the ground, thou shall not be established, nor thy kingdom. Wherefore now send and fetch him unto me, for he shall surely die. And Jonathan answered Saul his father, and said unto him, Wherefore shall he be slain? What hath he done? And Saul cast a javelin at him to smite him: whereby Jonathan knew that it was determined of his father to slay David. So Jonathan arose from the table in fierce anger, and did eat no meat the second day of the month: for he was grieved for David, because his father had done him shame."

Here we see two angry people. Saul was angry because he wanted to kill David but Jonathan had hidden him. Jonathan was angry because his father wanted to kill an innocent man. There are two types of anger here. One is an anger that is wicked and cruel, with no foundation at all. The second is the anger of a man who sees another man doing something evil. We shall study these types of anger later.

When Jonathan knew the mind of his father, he had to inform David, as they had agreed. David came out of the bush, the two of them embraced and they both wept. After this, Jonathan told him to go in peace while he went back to the palace.

YOU SHOULD AVOID ANGER

When King Saul was angry, he threw a javelin at his own son. If the javelin had hit Jonathan, he would have died instantly. When a man is angry, he can do all manner of evil things. As a matter of fact, an angry man is a mad man. Anger is actually a temporary madness. The Bible says in Ecclesiastes 7:9:

"Be not hasty in thy spirit to be angry: for anger resteth in the bosom of fools."

God gave me victory over anger the day I came across this passage. Any time someone wants to make me angry, I know their real desire is to make me become a fool. Therefore say that I refuse to become a fool. You should refuse to be a fool because the people God calls fools in the Bible are sinners. For example, the Bible says that The fool has said in his heart that there is no God. In another place, God calls fools those who fail to pay their vows. Proverbs 22:24-25 admonishes us not to befriend a fool:

"Make no friendship with an angry man: and with a furious man thou shalt not go; Lest thou learn his ways, and get a snare to thy soul"

Break your friendship with an angry man before he gets you into trouble. However, there is another type of anger. In Psalm 7:11, the Bible says:

"God judgeth the righteous, and God is angry with the wicked every day."

Although God can be angry against the wicked, He cannot be called a fool. God must have good reasons to be angry at the wicked. In other words, there is a kind of anger that you can almost call holy anger. In Mark 3:1-6, Jesus was in a synagogue and saw a man with a withered hand, which He healed. The Pharisees who were present complained because He had healed him on the Sabbath Day. The Bible says Jesus was angry with them.

There was another time when Jesus was angry, in Matthew 21:12-13. Jesus came into the temple and He saw men changing money in the house of God. He said they had turned the house of His Father into a den of robbers. He took a whip and chased them out of the place.

Ephesians 4:26-31 says we should be angry but sin not. You may wonder how one can be angry without sinning. The answer is when your anger is holy anger, but how do you know which anger is holy? If you are not sure it is better to stay away from all forms of anger.

In 2 Kings 3:13-15, Elisha was angry with good reason. An idol worshipping king came to him and said he wanted to find out about the future. Elisha told him to go and ask his father's idols. However, even during this holy anger, the

Holy Spirit left him because the Holy Spirit is a gentle dove. He had to ask a minstrel to sing in order to woo the Holy Spirit back. You must make up your mind that you will never be angry again.

In Number 20:2-12, we read that it was anger that kept Moses out of the Promised Land. Moses had been leading the children of Israel for forty years. He became angry for one day and God told him he would not enter the Promised Land.

Nobody gets angry without a cause. However, when somebody is trying to make you angry, you should know immediately that the enemy is trying to attack you. The enemy is trying to make you sin, but you should refuse to respond.

If you feel anger welling up within you, make sure you do not speak, because the moment you begin to speak, the anger begins to grow and before you know it, you could have said things that you would regret for the rest of your life.

When I married, I agreed with my wife that we must not get angry at the same time. Then the devil tried to trap us one day. We were travelling from Ilesha to Lagos. Something made her angry and I knew she was right. She had an opportunity to hit me for she was talking while I was driving. I was angry but I could not talk and there was no way of escape. When I could not control it anymore, in order not to break our rule, I parked the car, got down and began to walk back towards Ilesha. I left her with the baby in the car. After walking for about a mile, I arrived at a village where they were selling fruit and I bought some. I ate some and took the rest back to her in the car. By now she was frightened because she did not know what had happened. When she saw me coming, her anger turned to relief and as I got into the car, I gave her the peace offering.

Make up your mind today not to get angry again. I refuse to be a fool. James 1:19-20 says:

> *"Wherefore, my beloved brethren, let every man be swift to hear, slow to speak, slow to wrath: For the wrath of man worketh not the rightousness of God."*

Avoid anger at all cost.

GOD WILL NOT ACCEPT HALF MEASURES

If you want to follow Jesus, you must go all the way. Jesus will not accept half measures. In Revelation 3:15-16, He says:

> *"I know thy works, that thou art neither cold nor hot: I would thou were cold or hot. So then because thou art lukewarm, and neither cold nor hot, I will spue thee out of my mouth."*

God loves two categories of people. He loves those who love Him passionately. He also loves those who hate Him passionately because He will then work on them and turn them to friends. When those who have been great persecutors of Christians are converted, they always become very strong Christians. Saul of Tarsus wrote a third of the New Testament. He hated Christians and did not hide his hatred. He would grab them and throw them into prison. God loves these kinds of people because when you win them over to Jesus Christ, they become very strong Christians. But not all persecutors are saved!

The people that God hates are those who are half-hearted. God hates such people because they disgrace Him: In Luke 9:59-62, Jesus says that once you lay your hands on the plough, there is no looking back. In another place, in response to someone who wanted to follow Him but wanted to bury his dead father first, he said the dead should be left to bury the dead. Philippians 3:7-10 says:

> *"But what things were gain to me, those I counted loss for Christ. Yea doubtless, and I count all things but loss for the excellency of the knowledge of Christ Jesus my Lord: for whom I have suffered the loss of all things, and do count them but dung, that I may win Christ, And be found in him, not having mine own righteousness, which is of the law, but that which is through the faith of Christ, the righteousness which is of God by faith: That I may know him, and the power of his resurrection, and the fellowship of his sufferings, being made conformable unto his death;"*

I want to know the power of His resurrection and the fellowship of His sufferings. Many people want to know the power of his resurrection but they do not want the suffering that goes with it. Nobody will receive the power of God without suffering. If you want the power of His resurrection, you must have the fellowship of his suffering.

Many of us say 'Amen' to the prayer that we may do greater works than He has done, but what was the first work that He did? He fasted for forty days and forty nights. It was not raising of the dead that was the first work. He spent nights in prayer. The things that He did we should do also.

Jonathan followed David to the bush and went back to the palace. Likewise today, if you want to go on with Jesus Christ, you must be ready to go all the way: with the pleasure, power and the suffering. All of these must be rolled together. In Revelation 2:4, Jesus said we must be faithful unto death to receive the crown of life. In Acts 21:10-13, Paul said he was ready to be bound and die for Christ. No wonder he was so full of power.

In Luke 22:54-62, we read something interesting. When they came to arrest Jesus, the disciples fled. There was one man who did not run but neither did he stay too close to Jesus. His name was Peter. He followed afar off and soon found himself among those who were warming themselves, who recognised him as a disciple of Jesus Christ, whom he then denied knowing.

Paul said in Philippians 3:13-14:

> *"Brethren, I count not myself to have apprehended: but this one thing I do, forgetting those things which are behind, and reaching forth unto those things which are before, I press toward the mark for the prize of the high calling of God in Christ Jesus."*

We must keep pressing on, as Paul did. There must be no looking back. It is the same Paul that said in Romans 8:35-39 that nothing could separate him from the love of God. For him, it was to be Jesus all the way. Do not let anything stop you from following Jesus Christ all the way.

Notes